A TRANSPLANTED LIFE

My Story And Guide on Transplant Success

NOAH SWANSON

ISBN: 978-1-4834-3719-4 (sc)
ISBN: 978-1-4834-3718-7 (e)

Lulu Publishing Services rev. date: 11/05/2015

Dedicated to my dad, Lorris Alan Swanson

Contents

Foreword

Shakespeare introduced the concept (Hamlet IV, iii, 9-11) that:

"Diseases desperate grown, by desperate appliances are reliev'd, or not all."

This is particularly true for liver failure, for which is no treatment other than transplanting a new liver, one of the most difficult of all surgical procedures, and a very complex medical process. For those unfortunate enough to suffer liver failure, a liver transplant is a formidable undertaking. It requires an intensive team effort, and the patient and his or her family are important members of the team. Apart from the uncomfortable time of waiting for a donor while trying to stay alive despite a failing liver, a transplant is a daunting prospect, which when finally undertaken, has many components.

This is a story of *A Transplanted Life*, written through the eyes of a perceptive young person who has undergone and survived a liver transplant. Adolescence is difficult enough as it is, but imagine adding to it, facing up to a serious illness, facing death, and by some miracle or other, surviving. This book shares a story of survival through dark times, provides practical information for those and their families going through similar experiences, and makes an uplifting read for the rest of us.

Ross W Shepherd MD FRACP
Professor Emeritus
Formerly Medical Director, Pediatric Liver Transplantation at the University of Queensland, Washington University in St Louis, and Baylor College of Medicine, Houston.

A Mother's Heart

I have to admit that my expectations going into my son's transplant experience were a little unrealistic. However, being a mom with a very sick teenage son and having seen my husband go down this same road but lose his battle, may have had something to do with these expectations.

I was thinking, "Okay, this is June. Noah gets put on the list right away, gets his transplant, recovers, and is ready to start school in August." It sounded like a great plan in my book. Well, that's not how things were meant to be. Lyn, one of Noah's transplant coordinators, later told me that she had told Michelle, Noah's other coordinator, that she hoped I wouldn't be a problem to work with as the mother of a patient. She reminds me of it every time I see her. I soon discovered that the process was a little more complicated than I originally understood.

As our family waited with Noah during the last few moments before his surgery, my mind couldn't help but go back fourteen years earlier to the night of his dad's liver transplant. That night as I was walking with Lorry, Noah's father, to the elevator to go down to surgery, we ran into a couple of his transplant doctors who were carrying a cooler between them. Jokingly, I asked if they were transporting Lorry's liver. To my surprise, they answered, "Yes!" I have to admit, I wondered if we would see the same thing that night with Noah (but we didn't).

I remember how Noah didn't even seem nervous as he waited for his surgery. But having walked in these shoes before, I was the one who was nervous. I was worried because I was remembering the outcome of Lorry's transplant. But I was excited to think that this young man would be able to do the things he loved to do again. It was breaking my heart to see him sick; not feeling well, having to take naps and limiting his activity. I was also hopeful because I knew that Noah's situation was different from his dad's: the doctors had not let Noah's health deteriorate like his father's had leading up to his transplant. Because of this I was confident and I believed that God had a special purpose for Noah and He was going to do something very special in his life, beginning with a successful transplant. I was provided with a God-given peace and I could see that it was the same peace that Noah had as he waited.

In the early morning hours of August 26th, 2003, Noah's transplant team started the surgery that began a "new life" for him. After a few more hours, one of the doctors came out with an update. He explained how the scar tissue left behind from his previous surgery was making things a little more difficult. He compared it to chipping his arteries out of concrete. Because of this, the surgery was taking longer than expected but Noah was doing well.

As soon as they finished, Noah's transplant doctor, Dr. Shepherd, came out and said that Noah had done great and was in a recovery room. As I walked into the room, I remember how hard it was to see him for the first time. All I could think about was seeing his dad right after his surgery for the first time. He had been unable to speak because of the oxygen tube and was still sedated. I recalled how puffy Lorry looked and I worried I would walk in to see the same of my son. But when I saw Noah for the first time, he looked great! Sure, he was connected to tubes and had an arterial line in his neck, but he had a little bit of a smile. He was still waking up and was so glad to see us. For that, this mother's heart was overjoyed.

One of the first questions Noah asked was when he could get the line out of his neck; it bothered him. And the next question: when could he eat? He had just come out of a major operation and wanted to know when he could eat! We all thought it was so funny. He hardly ate anything in the weeks leading up to his surgery because of how sick he had become. He had lost over 25 lbs., so it was understandable why he was ready for something to eat. But his menu options were a moist, green sponge and ice chips for at least a day. Fortunately he was in the SICU for less than 24 hours and the doctors were amazed at his initial recovery.

My husband and a couple of Noah's siblings were able to stay for the first three days and then they had to return home. It was hard seeing them leave because their presence alone had been such an encouragement to Noah and helped lift his spirits.

After leaving the SICU, Noah was transferred to a private room which became our home for almost three months. Thankfully I was able to stay in Noah's room on a couch that doubled as a bed. I was able to remain near him most hours as the staff checked on him throughout the day.

To prevent sleep from becoming an even rarer commodity, I quickly learned how to silence the machine connected to his IV when it would start beeping. It would remain quiet long enough for the nurse to come in and check on it. I did my best to assist the nurses whenever they were away or had to step out of the room. Many times I was his arm extension when something was out of reach, such as a glass of water. As his mother, I felt blessed to be able to be there and participate in his care.

During the first days after his transplant, when he couldn't shower yet, we would "shampoo" his hair with a pre-packaged shampoo cap. Even though it wasn't the real thing, it helped him feel so much better. Sometimes just that small act alone gave him a more positive outlook on his situation.

A few days after the surgery the doctors discovered Noah's bile duct was leaking. It was a problem that needed to be taken care of immediately. A leaky bile duct wasn't completely uncommon, but it seemed that if there was something that could go wrong, it happened to Noah. It began to happen so often that it became a running joke: give Noah a million to one odds and it was going to happen. I'm thankful Noah was able to laugh at so many of these situations. His sense of humor often helped lighten otherwise difficult moments.

I was frequently on a mission to find whatever food he was craving. Whenever a certain food sounded good to him, I would do everything possible to get it. Because of the amount of weight he had lost, I knew how important it was that he consume enough calories each day. Many times the regular hospital food didn't sound good, so I would get him food from the hospital cafeteria and found myself making frequent trips to the Dairy Queen on the first floor of the hospital.

The hospital staff was also very accommodating and Noah was blessed with so many great nurses. If there was anything that they could bring him, his nurses were more than willing no matter what time of day. One night I didn't realize that Noah was having a difficult time sleeping until I woke up to find one of his nurses talking and praying with him.

And of course there was Noah's team of transplant doctors who came in each morning, usually six days a week with a smaller team on Sundays. They were so good with Noah and always explained everything as simply as possible. Each day after they left, Dr. Shepherd, along with Noah's transplant coordinators, would come back in to go over what had been discussed. Those three were key players in our hospital stay and well beyond into Noah's recovery. I can't say enough good things about them. Dr. Shepherd treated Noah like one of his own children. I'll never forget all the doctor visits in the years that followed when he would come in and sit right next to Noah on the examination table. Dr. Shepherd always had time to visit before doing Noah's assessment.

I never would have guessed what a key role Noah's coordinators would play in Noah's life and care. A transplant coordinator becomes one of your best friends... at least Noah's did. How thankful I am for these two ladies still to this day. No question was ever stupid and if they didn't know the answer, they would be diligent in finding it. One or both of them would be found in Noah's room several times a day checking in on him. Lyn trained us on Noah's meds and stressed the importance of being consistent in taking them. She wanted Noah to know why he was taking the medications he was on and how important they were for his health and recovery. I made many calls to these ladies the months after Noah left the hospital.

I didn't have a car throughout Noah's care in St. Louis, so every place I went had to be within walking distance. But I didn't want to be too far away, so it didn't bother me. Family and friends would often bring the necessities for Noah that I wasn't able to find nearby. I can't explain how much of an encouragement these visits were to both of us. Noah would especially look forward to the mail delivery when the nurses would deliver any cards or packages he had received that day. He was blessed with a pile of mail nearly every day and enjoyed opening his cards. These seemingly small acts of love really made a difference in keeping Noah's spirits high. There were still times along the path that he would get discouraged and want to speed up his healing process. But he and I both knew that there was a purpose for all that Noah was going through, even during those most difficult days.

The first twelve months out of transplant made for a tough year. The first three months were spent in St. Louis and the last three-quarters of the year back in Des Moines. There were many changes, many adjustments, many lab draws, and many times of feeling totally helpless in knowing what to do. But Noah never became bitter. It was a year of adjustments for Noah, myself, and our family, and I called Noah's transplant coordinators sometimes daily to ask them questions concerning almost anything about Noah's care. There was a lot to learn about how to keep this young man healthy. He had been in a hospital so much of the past two years that he had to adjust to what a normal, healthy lifestyle should be. Details such as developing a normal sleep pattern and being able to sleep through the night were hard at first, but Noah was on his way to a new life, and how thankful we were for that.

After one year out of transplant, we went back for a check-up. After being admitted for a few tests, Noah's two transplant coordinators came into the room to talk to us and gave us some of the results. They told us that Noah's disease was back in his new liver. What a blow that was to my heart. But the first thing Noah said to me was, "Mom, we knew this might happen." He took it so much better than I did. His response was an indication of how much he had grown through this journey. In that difficult moment, God used my son to minister to me. Immediately, the doctor started Noah on a medication that was meant to keep his disease in check, and it worked.

As time has passed, each year I try to make Noah's transplant anniversary a celebration because of the special event it marks in his life. I always remind Noah to never forget how special he is in God's eyes and never take for granted what God has done in his life, and continues to do. Noah has been given good health and now has a wonderful wife, Kara, to share his life with. His most recent blessing is their daughter, London Rae. This year we celebrated Noah's tenth year out of transplant!

Intro

"The best way out is always through."

-Robert Frost

I had just finished eighth grade when I began climbing the biggest mountain I had encountered in the first thirteen years of my life. However, before you begin to think I was a mountaineering prodigy, I confess that I'm unable to say I've scaled Mount Everest, K2, or any of the major peaks of the world. I've done my fair share of hiking and even climbed a couple smaller peaks. But I encountered this mountain in the rolling hills of Iowa. Those with any experience in the Midwest know that it is a predominately flat part of the country. But in spite of its surroundings, my mountain towered higher than I could have ever imagined.

In my little experience with mountain climbing, I had always imagined reaching the top of Mount Everest to be an unparalleled experience. I have a friend who has overcome Everest on more than one occasion. As an adventurer, Charlie admits that it's more about the journey itself than it is about reaching the top. He explains that the true reward is found within the introspective process between the base and the summit.

My Everest wasn't formed out of ice and rock. But, without a doubt, this uphill excursion was a test of strength and will. My mountain came in the form of a liver transplant. My journey through transplant provided mental, emotional, and physical challenges along the way. And after reaching the top I was provided with a beautiful view, but along the way I learned so much about who I am and the life I live.

Probably, like most of you, the sickness that led to transplant caught me completely off-guard. My father passed away from the same disease when I was two years old, but I never imagined I would be diagnosed with the same disorder. I was a teenager who rarely was sick when my doctors discovered something was wrong. After going through countless tests and procedures, I was blessed to receive a liver transplant three years later.

The goal of this book is two-fold. My first priority is to simply share my story with you. Through my story I want to let you into my mind, my thoughts, and emotions as I went through the organ transplant. I want to give you a glimpse of what this experience *could* look like for you. Not that you would compare your experience, but so that you could prepare for your own.

Secondly, I would like to be able to communicate what I learned through my journey in order to help you succeed in your own through practical advice. I am not a doctor. I am not a nurse. I do not intend to give you professional, medical advice. Everything I share with you comes from practical, personal experience. Through this book I hope to encourage you, answer some of the questions you may have, and provide you with a determination that will carry you through this journey.

Regarding the suggestions I make in this book, your doctor should first approve everything before you actively pursue them. There are pieces of advice I will offer as recommendations of what I found to help me through my personal journey. However, you should take every precaution that your doctors recommend. In addition to the medical advice your doctors give you, the suggestions I make are intended to help you be as successful as possible in your transplant experience. I hope and pray that everyone reading this book has the most uneventful, problem-free transplant possible.

I am revealing these things to you so that you might learn something from my experience to use along the path of your own journey. I will share with you the things that I learned through my experience, the things that I found that worked for me, and the things that did not work for me. It is far better to learn from someone else's mistakes than have to experience them for yourself.

PART 1

My Story

CHAPTER 1:
Stronger Cough Medicine

"The harder the conflict, the more glorious the triumph."

-Thomas Paine

Although I didn't get to spend much time with my father, I credit much of my success to values he instilled into me as a young boy. As I have grown, it has been a joy to discover many of the things we have in common. And many of the things I know of him today, I still hope to infuse into my character.

My father enjoyed working with his hands and he wasn't afraid to get dirty. He loved his family and led us well. His strength ran deep–physically, mentally, and spiritually. I've been able to see some of his patience and kind spirit in my older brother's personality according to those who knew my father best. In a conversation I once had with one of his closest friends, he described my father as being pound for pound the strongest man he knew.

My mom had a picture she used to keep in her Bible of a man hugging Jesus; one of those pictures you find in a bookstore that makes you feel nice and warm inside. In the picture, the man hugging Jesus has his back to you and from what I could tell it is what my father would have looked like from behind. In fact, for a long time I thought it was my father. Similar to the street artists at Disneyland, I figured Saint Peter was sitting at heaven's gate capturing these moments as people walked into Glory.

My father was an accountant for Winnebago, the big RV company based out of Iowa. He often spoke at our church when the pastor was away. Unfortunately, I received neither my father's way with numbers, nor his ability to speak in front of a crowd. I assume he was a little more left-brain than I could ever be. Shortly after my father passed away, my mother had my siblings and myself tested to make sure we didn't have the same disease that my father had. Both my brother and sister's tests came back negative, but mine came back a little abnormal. Different enough that it caused the doctors to want to re-run the test. However, the second time the test was run everything seemed to look fine. So, I guess, that was that. I didn't have the disease my father had. I'm sure my mom was happy to know that of all the things that I did not share in common with my father that this was one of them.

I never really gave much thought to the sickness that took my father away from me during the early years of my life. Until I stepped through the doorway of my teen years I hadn't experienced much sickness. But when I was thirteen I caught a cold that just would not go away. At first, I blamed it on allergies and assumed that with time it would clear up. By the time I gave it the attention it deserved, the cold had been lingering like an uninvited guest for nearly three months. We were about to go away for the weekend to my aunt and uncle's lake house, and my mom decided if nothing else, it at least called for a stronger cough medicine.

Before leaving for the weekend, she demanded I see our family doctor. I assured her that it was not necessary to see a doctor for a cold, but decided to go along with the idea to appease her motherly concern. *It's just a cold,* I remember saying to myself.

Reluctantly, I took my seat in the waiting room and began thumbing through the pages of the nearest magazine while my mom checked me in. Three magazines and half of a soap opera later, a nurse came through the door as she had done several times before. Sitting in a doctor's office against my will during summer break was not my idea of a good time. Thankfully, this time as she looked up from her clipboard called out, "Noah Swanson." Following her through the maze of hallways that made up the back half of the clinic she led me into an exam room. After placing a Popsicle stick on my tongue and jabbing her needlepoint flashlight in my ear, she asked me to describe the reason for my doctor appointment. I probably pointed to parental concern as my reason for being there. Making a few notes in a file, she walked towards the door and assured me that my doctor would be in momentarily to see me.

It was one of the things I had always appreciated about this doctor; he did not seem to keep his patients waiting long. Shortly after walking through the door he began to run his own diagnostics, feeling my neck and stomach, and checking my reflexes. He had removed allergies from the possible contributing factors. The doctor then ordered a few blood tests to be run, followed by an x-ray of my chest. As a teenage boy, the minutes seemed to drag by like years as I waited in the doctor's office. I wanted to be at my aunt and uncle's lake house with a cold, sugary drink in my hand soaking up the heat of another Midwest summer. As far as I was concerned, this time I was spending with the doctor was only eating away at the time I could have been swimming in the lake. With a weekend full of fun in the sun ahead of me and a junior high sized attention span, my mind had all but checked out.

By the time the doctor walked back in to the room, my impatience had begun to transform into concern. From the look on my mom's face, I could sense the worry growing inside her mind. After what felt like an entire summer's worth of waiting, the doctor came back into the room and asked us to come look at the x-rays with him. I didn't know what I was looking at, I had never seen an x-ray, but I sensed something was not right. As the doctor began to explain what we were seeing, my thoughts began to turn into frustration and despair. My hopes for a weekend in the sun soon sunk down into the pit of my stomach as the doctor explained to me that all of the clusters of white dots revealed a bad case of pneumonia, accompanied by what looked like mono.

Even still, my doctor wasn't satisfied with the prognosis. Something didn't add up and he wanted me to see a specialist as soon as possible. As I continued to stare at the white spots on the x-ray, the thought circled in my mind, *this type of thing doesn't happen to me!*

In these moments my mind wavered between "what if" and denial. *What if the doctors find something worse than pneumonia?* And then my mind wandered further down that path… *what if they find something terribly wrong? What if it is cancer? What if it's something even worse than that? Is there something worse than that?* It is the type of thought process that leaves you with your jaw wide open and your hand clasped over your mouth as if you've seen a terrible vision.

In spite of all these dramatic conclusions my mind began to draw, I quickly shook it off and convinced myself it was no big deal. I reassured myself with these-types-of-things-only-happen-to-other-people kind of thinking. I kept my chin up knowing that most likely it would all end up becoming a crazy story to share the next year of school.

As we walked out of the clinic, back into the light of the late morning sun, I self-medicated myself with a dose of positive thinking: *It could be worse,* I thought. *Most likely just a one-day set back. It's a mistake… just a big misunderstanding. It will all end in a sigh of relief… I'm sure of it,* I convinced myself. *After all, it is most likely just pneumonia. So I'll probably have to get some antibiotics, take it easy for a week, and miss a day at the lake. Life will carry on.* My mom made the call to my aunt to tell her we wouldn't make it that night.

A summer to remember

On the way home from the doctor's office, as I sat alone in my thoughts, again, my mind began to flood with worry, irritation, and anxiety. I feared the "what if" but what if what? I didn't know exactly what I should be worried about. *Is this what the beginning of the road looks like for a cancer patient?* I couldn't help but wonder. No one in my family had ever had cancer. I had never gone to see the doctor and left without an answer.

Other than the week I spent in the hospital for a ruptured spleen, the only time I visited the doctor was for an annual sports physical. I had never even broken a bone for that matter. I was active, I loved playing sports, and I had always been healthy but for the occasional cold.

The next day my mom took me to see the specialist. As we walked across the parking lot through the sweltering summer heat, beads of sweat quickly began to form on my brow. The layer of black top covering the parking lot made it feel like I was walking through an oven. We made our way towards the front doors and found our way to the front desk.

I took my seat in the waiting area and immediately felt out of place. *I'm not sick–I feel great! Sick kids belong here, not me.* The thought went around and around in my mind like a scrolling banner. That thought coupled with the fact I was sitting in a "children's" hospital made me feel even more out of place. I was less than three months away from entering my freshman year in high school; I was a thirteen-year-old man as far as I was concerned. Instead of Sports Center on the TV and Sports Illustrated scattered across the table, there were cartoon shows, grade school magazines, and children's building blocks strewn about. I was already irritated by the lack of answers from the previous day's appointment, so all I wanted, at this point, was to see this specialist, for him to tell me everything looked okay, and to move on with my summer plans.

Sooner than I expected a nurse came to get my mother and me. She recorded my temperature, height, weight, and blood pressure, then led me into a colorful room with smiling animal cartoons covering the walls. I hate to admit, but if I was going to be stuck in a hospital, the bright colors and happy animals seemed to help a little. Shortly after finding my seat atop the exam table the doctor walked in. After a few moments of small talk, the doctor asked me to explain, in my own words, what was going on, and how I had been feeling. He then gave us a brief synopsis from the notes that he had received explaining the situation to make sure we were all on the same page.

Once it was confirmed we were all tracking together, he pulled out my file and began to talk me through its contents. He thumbed through the pages almost as if he was looking at everything for the first time. As he looked up at me I noticed his eyes were void of the certainty that usually exists before a doctor issues a diagnosis. I was used to a doctor looking at me and saying something like, "Yep, it's a cold. Take this prescription to your pharmacy to get it filled, take it easy, and come back in two weeks if you aren't feeling any better." But his eyes did not display that type of confidence.

"Well, you don't have mono… but you do have pneumonia. However, I am not sure what the underlying issue is."

It was not the response I was hoping for. I had come into this doctor's office fully expecting to get a black and white diagnosis of what was going on, along with the remedy of how to fix it. As he continued to talk with us, he spoke of what he did know and the possibilities of what could be going on in order to prepare.

This was the first time in my journey that I felt my curiosity turn into something more than anxiety or frustration. This was the first time in the culmination of these two seemingly inconclusive appointments that I felt fear. Until now, the hopeful curiosity had kept me anxiously waiting for the answer to what was going on. I sat listening as he talked us through some of the things that could be causing the symptoms and the possible outcomes.

I can still remember the one I heard the loudest. I didn't just hear the word; I felt the word fly through the air and explode against my chest, cutting through me like a surgeon's scalpel. Although the doctor was mild-mannered and soft-spoken, the word dropped out of his mouth like a grenade: cancer!

"There is the possibility that this could be cancer. It's something we have to be prepared for."

Cancer? This was my first big dose of reality that rattled my world. A reality I swallowed like a spoon full of the most bitter cough medicine imaginable. I hardly heard the qualifying words "slight possibility" before the doctor had mentioned cancer. In that moment, I might as well have been given a death sentence. For the first time in my short life I knew what it meant to see my life flash before my eyes.

At the end of the appointment a wave of nervous frustration washed over me. I realized I hadn't taken any steps closer in discovering what was going on inside my body. I didn't understand what was happening to me, my parents didn't understand, my doctor didn't understand, and now even the specialist couldn't understand what was happening.

I don't know if it was an act of despair or an exercise in positive thinking, but I quickly lost myself inside my imagination. As silly as it may sound, I found myself conjuring up the idea of an undiscovered super power. As a thirteen-year-old boy with a comic book collection and a wild imagination, I hoped I was experiencing something similar to Peter Parker when he was bitten by the spider in the Spider Man comic. Maybe this was just a super-human, genetic-altering event going on inside my body. Of course, it was not one of the possibilities that the doctor had discussed with me. But I liked to think that maybe the idea was not so far off.

In my limited life-experience, I tried to keep a grasp of what was going on around me. I was fighting to keep my mind and my emotions from unraveling. If it meant escaping reality but for a moment, then that was what I had to do. But, in that moment I do not know if I would say I felt super-human. Uneasy? Yes. Frustrated? Yes. But in spite of my nervous frustration, I could not help but think that maybe the doctors had it wrong. *Maybe those were someone else's X-rays; maybe those blood work results were someone else's too. Maybe they misread the results. And maybe this is all a big misunderstanding.*

I sure didn't feel sick. Especially not sick enough to have two doctors already in this process and still have no clear answer. As my mind desperately raced to make sense of what was happening, I could not help but continue to entertain such thoughts. All the while my mind toed a line between fear and doubt. I feared what lay ahead. I feared what the doctors would discover was making me sick. Maybe it was my teenage naivety, but I couldn't help but doubt as well. I doubted that this was even happening. My world as I knew it, at that moment, was being rocked in a way I never knew possible. At this early stage in my journey, I was still ignorant to the severity of what lay ahead.

The specialist decided to transfer me on to a different specialist within the same hospital. And this was not much comfort to me. As we left the doctor's office I began to wonder if they would ever find what was going on. Now two doctors could not figure out what was going on inside of my body. *Does that even happen?* I wondered. One doctor, maybe, but now two?

CHAPTER 2:
My Life as a Human Test Subject

*"The first step toward success is taken when you refuse to
be captive of the environment in which you find yourself."*

-Mark Caine

A toxic cocktail: my concern mixed with fear, as questions seemed to pile
up while answers remained scarce. I did not know what was going on, the
specialists I was being tossed around to did not seem to know what was
going on either, and I did not feel like we were getting any closer to finding
an answer. *Isn't that what specialists are supposed to do?* I would ask myself.
If they aren't finding the answers, who in the world will?

It wasn't mono; my doctors had ruled that out. I did have pneumonia
however, but it was not the culprit behind the strange lab results. The
doctors had crossed off a couple other options as well, but what was next?
There were times I thought that maybe I would turn out to be some medical
mystery. Maybe an intriguing topic for one of *20/20's* documentaries: *The
Undiagnosed Thirteen-Year-Old Boy.* Or maybe I would find myself taking
a journey to the ends of the earth in search of a remedy. Maybe I would
discover a secluded monk, or a wise old sage who would hold a cure to my
ailment. In that scenario I imagined myself climbing to the top of a near
endless mountain of cobbled steps to drink a terrible tasting elixir that
would instantaneously heal me.

I sank back into my reality as the next week brought about the next appointment with the next specialist. I was beginning to see an uncomfortable pattern. As we made our way back to the hospital, I hoped this would be the end of it: a straightforward diagnosis with a medication and the necessary steps in order to get better. Going to the doctor to begin with, just a few days earlier, was more than I was comfortable with. But now I was two doctors deeper into the cycle and already tired of it. *Is there a light at the end of this tunnel I am going down?* I couldn't help but wonder. Less than a week of searching for my diagnosis, I was tired.

Again the nurse called me back and motioned me into the doctor's exam room, however, this time she seemed to stray from the usual list of demands. "Please remove your pants and wait for the doctor to come in and see you."

Wait... what? At that moment, the whole experience jumped up ten more points on the uncomfortable scale. I was thirteen, and the "turn and cough" phrase was something we joked about in the locker rooms after having our yearly sports physicals. But I had already had my sports physical. Why on earth did I need to drop my pants at this point?

But in the name of medicine, if this is going to help these docs find my problem, I won't stand in the way, I conceded. I was not about to delay the process of solving this mystery. A lesson I quickly learned from this experience: an honest, open relationship was truly the best relationship I could have with my doctor. A doctor's exam room was no place for secrecy.

Sitting on the edge of the exam table, pants around my ankles, I was feeling about as awkward as possible. But shortly after the doctor arrived I found myself sitting much more comfortably with my pants back around my waist. I guess it was just part of the elimination process. We talked through much of the same information the prior specialist had walked me through.

I was now reaching the point of nearly automated responses when each routine question was asked from each doctor. After checking off each of his questions with each of my answers, he proceeded to run a few of his own tests. Setting his file folder down, he asked me to lie on my back.

"Now lay on your stomach. Now roll onto your side. Now cough for me. Again. And one more time, please. Now stand up for me. Bend your arm."

This was how the interactive portion of the doctor appointments would go. With all the poking and prodding I was beginning to feel a little bit like a human test subject. Both mentally and physically my health was analyzed, one glass slide at a time, under the doctor's microscopic inspection. With each appointment, blood draw, and procedure I hoped, if nothing else, it would bring me one step closer to a diagnosis. At times, while going from one test to the next, I began to feel my hope expiring from what seemed like an endless path of indirection.

More blood work was ordered; more tests were run. As the process moved forward, symptoms were considered, lab results were evaluated and slowly the signs began to point to my liver as the culprit. Answers were still forthcoming, but something was going on inside my liver that wasn't supposed to be.

With this discovery came my first operation: the first of many liver biopsies. It was one more step that I took going deeper into the reality I was still trying to ignore. But avoiding this reality was about as useless as ignoring the kid sitting in front of you who refused to shower after P.E. class. For a moment you may be able to close your eyes and pretend he's not there, but the evidence of his presence still lingers in the air.

And so, I swallowed my next dose of reality. The doctor ordered that a sample be taken of my liver in order to analyze its current state. He explained that they were going to put me to sleep and use a big, long needle to grab a sample.

With this first procedure, I found myself moving closer to embracing this reality that existed around me. I am not sure if it was deliberate or if I simply had not yet taken the time to stop and process everything. For the first several weeks I had been living with a sense of ignorance. In the back of my mind I still hoped all the chaos and bad news would eventually go away. But for the first time, I was beginning to accept the truth that this was, in fact, actually happening to me. But I wasn't ready to accept it entirely. Like an out of body experience, I was watching everything take place from a comfortable distance, not taking ownership of what was happening. Until I had my first biopsy, I wasn't exactly sure what I was supposed to respond to, let alone how I should be responding. Sure, I felt fear. But it was a fear of the unknown. And I was anxious. But the anxiety was focused on all the uncertainty.

The procedure was scheduled for Monday, July 23rd, 2001. The night before the biopsy I remember thinking to myself, *I'm actually going to have a surgery!* The thought brought with it a curious anxiety, although the term "surgery" seemed a little severe for what the procedure actually was.

After the biopsy I woke up with a little soreness around the left side of my ribs. My doctor assured me that they were able to collect a good sample during the biopsy and would know more just as soon as the lab results came back.

Throughout this time I tried to maintain an attitude that all was well; still holding on to somewhat of a blissful ignorance to all that was happening; still towing the line between denial and reality. As I started to shuffle through the stories my mother had so often shared with me about my father, the caring father he was to my siblings and me, the loving husband he had been, and also of the sickness that ultimately took him away from us, I began to discover the similarities my father and I shared. I may not have acquired his financial wit or his calm personality, but I would soon find that he and I would share a very similar journey. My path would not end at the same place as my father's, but I would share an experience with him that my siblings did not have the opportunity to understand.

The results from the biopsy proved to affirm what the previous doctor had suspected. The problem sat within my liver. The outcome of the biopsy prompted the doctors to transfer my care yet again, to the hepatologists at the University of Nebraska Hospital in Omaha. After several months of labs, procedures, and what seemed like one doctor after another, I felt like I was beginning to see a glimmer of a light at the end of the tunnel. However, the light was revealing a truth that I was not sure I wanted to know. The reality began to set in: *I really am sick* I began to realize.

Symptoms

Until this time, my symptoms had not been connected to a diagnosis, giving little inclination as to what was taking place inside my body. But it was not before long that the unmistakable signs of liver failure began to reveal themselves. A bloated stomach was the first indication to give way. My liver was swollen, my spleen continued to enlarge, and fluid had begun to collect in my abdomen. Not exactly the combination I was looking to show off at the pool that summer.

As an active kid growing up, naps had never been my favorite activity. I could usually find better ways of utilizing my time. But as time progressed, that suddenly began to change. I soon found myself becoming exhausted by the middle of the afternoon in desperate need of rest. Shortly after the continual fatigue set in, I began to notice further symptoms manifesting themselves.

While brushing my teeth one evening, I took a look into my own, tired eyes and noticed a new development. I had grown accustom to my eyes not looking quite as vibrant as they once were. But now, for the first time, there was a discoloration in the whites of my eyes. The rim around my eyes, once white and clear, begun to discolor into a yellowish hue.

Shortly before I was transferred on to Omaha, my doctors in Des Moines began a daily medication schedule. I still laugh at my younger self when I recall the time my doctor handed me the prescriptions to take to the pharmacist. I thought, *How cool! This is kind of like the movies when the hero gets knocked down and someone else comes along, reaches into his coat pocket, hands him his medication, and he's instantaneously brought back to his feet: like a bolt of energy running through his body.*

Once again, my ignorance and reality would meet head—on, with reality coming out the clear winner. What I did not know was that I would be taking more than one prescription at a time: there would be many, many more. My doctor did not just hand me one prescription to go fill; he handed me a stack of them. It's not exactly practical carrying around seven bottles of pills in your pocket. For me, the movie scene would have gone something like this: I get knocked to the ground, my trusty sidekick comes to my aide, but instead of handing me one, magic pill, he is required to provide me with a gym bag full of pills. Not exactly the Hollywood cut I had in mind.

Side effects

I don't recall the side effects of each drug. However, the one that brought about the most memorable side effect was clearly Prednisone. Many of you are probably familiar with this medication. And you are also probably already aware that today's energy drinks have nothing on the energy this prescription provides (at least in larger doses). I went from hardly being able to stay awake to hardly being able to go to sleep. I felt like someone had strapped a battery pack to my back like the Energizer Bunny.

I was first introduced to Prednisone in a small dose, so I was not yet aware of all the side effects. When I first started taking the medication I had some acne breakouts. I wasn't crazy about that, but I could handle it. But then out of nowhere came an inexhaustible amount of energy. I didn't know if I loved it or hated it. Two to three hours of sleep became my normal sleep schedule most nights. Then I started to gain a little weight. At the time, I weighed just a little more than the baggy jeans that hung from my waist, so I could tolerate the few extra pounds as well.

I attended a very small, private high school. At the beginning of each school year, the entire high school would go away for two nights to a camp. Our school rented out the cabins and the rest of the camp's facilities while we were there. My first year was one of my most memorable only because I didn't get any sleep. Watching TV, sketching, and raiding the refrigerator were my standard late night sleep aide. Unfortunately, staying in a cabin without a TV, electricity, or a fully stocked refrigerator I was without that remedy. I quickly discovered that staring at the underside of a bunk bed did not suffice. The only other option I had to get myself to fall asleep was to talk to anyone that would listen. My best friend from high school, and unsuspecting bunkmate, became the unfortunate victim of my insomnia over the next two days. After too many sleepless nights I clearly made up my mind that my newly discovered energy was great during the day, but horrible during the night. And with that, my doctors added a sleep aide to my list of medications.

Another side effect I faced throughout this time was cramps. I wasn't sure if they were from one of my medications or the result of something else going on inside my body. Usually they would occur somewhere in my legs, and without warning, they would burrow deep into the muscle and, consequently, launch me to my feet.

Unfortunately, these cramps did not occur at the most opportune times. And I certainly didn't enjoy the extra attention received from jumping up and down to shake out the cramp. But I meant it when I said I had no other option than to leap to my feet. One of the most memorable cases took place five rows from the front of a movie theatre during the middle of a movie. Unsuspectingly eating my popcorn and sipping my soda, out of nowhere my right hamstring tightened up like a rubber band ready to be sent across the room. It would have been fitting if I had been watching *Saving Private Ryan, Braveheart,* or any other inspirational movie. But it was a teenage comedy undeserving of a standing ovation.

Instantly I jumped up as if a surge of electricity was flowing through my seat. Apparently everyone thought I was doing some mid-movie stretching, because other than a couple of strange looks, no one said a word.

Another memorable cramp attack I recall took place on a long ride home from Colorado. Since I was the smallest of the group, and apparently the easiest to fit into tight spaces, I was relegated to sitting in the far back recesses of the SUV. Surrounded by luggage, skis, and an ice chest, I sat comfortably for about one out of the twelve hours of the ride home. But like so many times before, a cramp seized the back of my leg. Without anywhere to go I catapulted myself over the tops of everyone's heads to the front of the vehicle. In a SUV filled with grown men, this was not comfortable for anyone. Thankfully my sympathetic brother-in-law obliged my need to walk it off and franticly pulled to the side of the road the first chance he had.

Omaha

Life with a failing liver was never boring. From random cramps to terrible tasting contrast. They say smell is the sense most closely connected to memory, but I believe taste is a close second. Just thinking about it causes my mouth to salivate. It looked like milk, but tasted like poison. Hovering over the garbage can, I choked down each mouthful, fighting my body's urge to vomit it back out. This was not my first CT scan (CT stands for computed tomography and it is sometimes referred to as a "cat" scan), but it hadn't become any easier to gag down the contrast I was required to drink before the exam (the liquid you consume prior to a CT scan in order to make your internal organs appear on the monitor–it works as a "highlighter" for your organs). It didn't make sense to me that with all the advances in modern medicine, why on earth the stuff you were required to drink before a CT scan still tastes so terrible. If dentists had found a way to make fluoride taste like marshmallows then why weren't they able to find a way to make the contrast formula half way tolerable? The last time I had a CT scan the administering nurse was kind enough to mix it with Sprite. However, it hardly masked the taste, and now every time I drink Sprite I think of that awful taste.

It had been several months since I visited my doctor to remedy what I thought was a cold. Since that doctor appointment, I had seen the inside of more doctors' offices than I care to remember. Next stop on the journey: Omaha, Nebraska. As my symptoms became more prevalent, my ignorance continued to awaken to a sharp reality. The mantra that had played repeatedly in my mind, *this isn't happening to me... this isn't happening to me,* was soon replaced by the truth that this was, indeed, happening to me. A truth I was being forced to take ownership of.

Further from home, but closer to finding my answers, I had my first appointment at the University of Nebraska Medical Center. I had enjoyed visiting their zoo as a boy, but I never had any desire to visit their hospital. As we had done several times before, my mom and I mapped our way through another hospital complex to the office of my scheduled appointment and I took my seat in the waiting area until I was called back to the examination room. After my vital signs had been taken, I once again found my place upon, yet another paper-adorned exam table. Transfixed, I sat anticipating the meeting with the doctor who would undoubtedly discover the solution.

Dr. Horslen was a reserved yet direct doctor who seemed to usher in a sense of tranquility as he entered the room. As he introduced himself to me and laid out the process he would begin to initiate, I quickly noticed that his English accent did not contain any of the uncertainty I had heard in the voice of the other doctors up to this point. Like an accomplished explorer, he charted a course to guaranteed discovery. An expert in his field of study, he was confident, certain of the road that lay before us. He assured me that he would find the answers I had been looking for. As he sat on the stool before me, I felt a confidence similar to the one I got on the playground when I realized I was on the same team as the biggest kid in school. At that moment, I felt like I was on the winning team.

He first told me of the tests he would run and then briefly spoke of a few possibilities I could anticipate. To begin the process, he called for his own panel of blood work to be drawn. At the same time, he ordered that another CT scan be conducted followed by a biopsy. By this time, I had begun to realize that whatever was taking place inside my body would most likely require more than a quick fix. But I still didn't know what that would look like, and for me, these were uncharted waters. I was trapped within an endless labyrinth of tests and procedures. Through this time of "wait and see" my life seemed like it had come to a standstill and I felt as though I was sitting in a grounded plane on the runway waiting to take flight.

Much of the mystery would soon be dissolved because after my first biopsy in Omaha my diagnosis was discovered. A few days after the blood work results had been brought back and the outcome of the biopsy had been determined, my doctor diagnosed me with Type 1 autoimmune hepatitis. According to the American Liver Foundation, it is, "A chronic disease in which the body's own immune system attacks the liver and causes it to become inflamed." In the simplest way possible, my doctor explained that my body was attacking its own liver.

As a teenager, that didn't make sense to me. *Well, that's just stupid,* I thought. *Isn't my body supposed to work together? Why in the world would it try to kill one of its own organs? Can't we just force it to get along?* As if my body's organs were a group of unruly teammates.

In situations that were more frustrating than usual, I found the most effective thing to do was to break it down in a way I could understand it better; something I was more comfortable with. But even then, I often found myself floating out of the situation just for a moment. Up out of the sickness, above the pain, and constant doctor's appointments to think about what it would be like if none of this had ever happened. To think again, just for a moment, if this was all a bad dream. It hadn't been long since my sickness had been discovered, but even in this short time it had become a way of life. This was my reality. This was happening to me, and I learned to accept this new awareness and say, "I'm going through this, but, by the grace of God, it won't get the best of me!"

Fear

The first three-fourths of my high school experience was anything but typical. Not only was I working through the usual teenage personal identity dilemma, I was also trying to figure out what was happening to my body other than puberty. While my friends were concerned about what clothes to where to school, I was concerned if my clothes would cover the drainage bags that hung from my stomach. *Would I always be this way? Would I always be sick and fatigued? Would I always stare into the yellow eyes I saw each morning in the mirror? Was this my new normal?*

The anxious feelings of fear would often creep up and grab me by the throat. Even during the most mundane activities of the day, the cold, icy fingers of fear would grip me in its clutches if I allowed.

Webster defines fear as, "an unpleasant often strong emotion caused by anticipation or awareness of danger." Fear can be either debilitating, or it can be motivating. It can be a bad thing, but it can also be a good thing because fear serves a purpose. At first, I struggled greatly with the fear and anxiety I experienced. The fear of being different, the fear of the unknown, and the fear of the pain I experienced with certain procedures.

As children we are taught to fear. It is not something we are born with. "Don't touch the stove because it is hot" or, "don't stick your finger in the electrical socket because it will shock you." We are not born with knowledge of the properties of heat; neither do we know anything about the characteristics of electrical currents. My daughter as a one year old, reminded me of the ignorance we all likely possessed as an infant. In the short time she had been on the earth, she hadn't learned to fear. When she would play on the bed, she would walk to the edge without concern of the consequences of falling off head first.

At an early age, most children have not yet personally experienced the pain these events can provide. That pain is what in turn teaches us to fear the repercussions associated with the dangers around us. This is a healthy fear and is essential to life. A fear of what does us harm only proves to protect us. We fear pain, but pain is what teaches us to fear.

We also fear the unknown. As a child, I can still remember the fear I experienced every time I walked down the stairs into our basement. After a few steps the staircase turned, and at the bottom of the next set of stairs was a set of cupboards above a countertop. Across from the countertop was a little window near the ceiling. The way the light of the window was cast against the countertop caused a strange shadow to appear against the wall. My wild imagination didn't help, and each time I reached the bottom of those stairs I was greeted by the shadow of a large man with an enormous nose.

It was several years before I realized where the shadow was coming from, and until that time, I worried some strange man with a giant nose would jump out from somewhere. I've discovered that one of the greatest ways to conquer fear is to eliminate the unknown if possible. There are certain unknowns that will remain a mystery, but there are others that can be exposed. In my experience with the basement as a little boy, it required that I stop and realize where the shadow was coming from. However, I was not comfortable enough to analyze what was causing the shadow until my older brother was with me late one afternoon. As we walked down the stairs together I was emboldened to rationally asses the situation and see that there was no large-nosed man lurking in my basement, but rather a couple of strange angles and a counter top creating the shadow.

Throughout my journey fear and dread came in all shapes, sizes, and even flavors. As my medical care continued on at the University of Nebraska Medical Center, my high school career carried on as well. While my treatment continued I would schedule regular appointments with my doctor in Omaha still doing regular blood work back in Des Moines so that my doctors could constantly monitor my progress. In order to get a more detailed look at my progress, whether good or bad, my doctor scheduled different tests to be run.

There was one specific test during this time that I seem to remember better than the rest. It was the first CT scan I had while receiving care in Omaha. As I previously stated, it wasn't my first CT scan, so I had prepared myself for the terrible tasting contrast I would be forced to ingest before they could administer the test. One of the ways I learned to overcome worry was to look at each thing I dreaded as an opportunity for success. Something I would conquer rather than be conquered by.

As requested, I arrived a half-hour early to the scheduled exam in order to drink the required amount of contrast and have time to let it set for a while before the CT scan was conducted. I'm not sure why I continue to ask the question, but as always, I asked the nurse, "Does this contrast have a bad taste?"

"No, it doesn't taste that bad," the nurse replied.

Apparently "bad" was a relative definition. The description could not have been any more inaccurate. Until that point, I had consumed my fair share of CT scan contrast, and it never tasted good, but this was by far the worst. Never before had it caused me to lose my lunch. This contrast wasn't even clear. It was milky white and came in a prepackaged capsule-like container. What they gave me looked like something they might drink on a spaceship. Before cracking the bottle's seal I questioned whether it was even the correct liquid. By this time I had been around a few hospitals and I knew what this stuff normally looked like: this was not it. But the nurse assured me that it was the right stuff.

I then proceeded to make my first mistake: I began by taking a little sip. I immediately gagged. It tasted terrible and I began to consider my options. "I could throw it all in the trash and say that I drank it. Or I could just drink part of it and throw the rest away."

I recalled, from one of my previous CT scans, a nurse explaining that the CT scan would not work if I did not consume the contrast prior to the scan. With that thought, I immediately began drinking it again. The fear of needlessly going through this process once again forced me to continue slurping down the milky white liquid. I wasn't about to have to come back in for another appointment. In that brief moment, I quickly realized that I really didn't have any options at all. The sooner I drank the stuff, the sooner I could get done with the test and the sooner I could get out of there.

Then it became a matter of strategy. Slow and steady sips or large gulps of the opaque solution? I took one big, long drink and pulled the canister from my lips. Immediately, my stomach did a summersault and my mouth began to water. I ran to the trashcan and was reintroduced to last night's dinner. My strategy was not working as well as I had hoped.

As I looked up from the trashcan, I was hoping to receive some sympathy. I may have received some pity if I had been with my mom, instead it was my sister who was there to give me some much-needed motivation; a kick to the pants; a one-phrase pep talk: "If you just drink it, you can get it over with." She could not have been more correct. I heeded the advice and went back to work.

I was determined that this would not get the best of me. So I tried the exact same thing as before, but this time I did it while holding my nose, and... same result. So I gave up on "strategy" and put a new plan in place: stand over the garbage, drink the contrast as quickly as possible, and try to keep as much of it down as I could. I think more of it ended up at the bottom of the trashcan than in my stomach. Apparently the amount that I was able to hold down did its job and they were able to complete the procedure. In the end that was all that mattered to me.

Following the proper steps as instructed by my doctors always proved to be the best choice for my healthcare. That meant making sure to complete the tests that my doctors ordered such as CT scans and blood work. It also meant making sure to follow the dietary restraints they would offer. When asked what advice he would offer to patients going through a transplant, Dr. Simon Horslen simply advised, "Remember to do the things you are supposed to do." This advice may sound elementary, but it is not always the easiest advice to follow. Especially when the direction provided by your doctor is neither enjoyable, nor easy to follow.

I have often been told that "too much of a good thing is a bad thing." Well, if that is the case, then too much of a bad thing is a very, very bad thing. Take fast food for example; although very tasty it tends to lack in nutritional value. I realize this isn't anything you don't know already. However, as a teenager, I had an obsession with a particular fast food chain. I was a loyal, constantly consuming fan of their chicken platters with an extra side of hush puppies.

In high school, I was a little skinnier than I would have preferred, and now that I was ill, I was having a harder time maintaining my weight. With that in mind, I thought I would put my metabolism to the test. With such a consistent diet of deep fried chicken the first question that might come to your mind might be, "How much weight did you gain?" And my answer would be, "I'm not sure." It wasn't my weight that was negatively impacted by these habits. It was my health.

Throughout this time, my doctors were monitoring my health too closely to allow anything to get too out of control. Soon after I had begun this new, deep fried diet they began to notice a change in the fluids they were monitoring.

"Have you made a change to your diet?" my doctor asked during one of my regular appointments. Curiously, I responded with my own question: "Why do you ask?"

"The fluids we've been monitoring are thickening and becoming discolored. What have you been eating?" I was ashamed to answer the question. I liked my fast food, but not enough to cost me my health. My body was having a hard enough time without my excessive fast food consumption making it worse.

I made the adjustment to my diet, cut out the fast food, but my health continued to deteriorate. My doctors decided to take a more aggressive plan of action. My body was not responding to the medications the way they had hoped it would. However, they weren't ready to place me on the donor list just yet. They had one more option before going down that road. The doctors told me I would be undergoing a splenorenal shunt in order to alleviate some of the stress on my liver. I had no idea what they were even talking about. I wasn't even sure they were speaking English. But there was one thing I was sure of: this was my second big dose of reality. As my doctor began to explain the procedure, my heart sunk as I realized this would require much more than a needle poke.

From the beginning, this was what I prayed I would avoid. I sat in a cloud of anger, frustration, and shock as my doctor described the operation. He was going to detach a couple veins here and reattach them over there in order to make things flow better. Or at least that was what I gathered from the explanation.

His words seemed to be muted during those next few moments as I sat there, alone in my thoughts. I remember staring at the wall thinking to myself, *They're going to have to open me up.* I may not have understood the exact details of the procedure at first, but I understood the doctor very clearly when he described the incision they would be making across my abdomen. Until now, I had just been poked and prodded. The most major operation I had faced until now was a biopsy. The only pain I felt with that was a little soreness on my side from where the biopsy needle had entered. And other than small discomfort, the only mark it left was a small needle-sized hole near my ribs. But this was a whole different thing.

How big will the scar be? How long will I have to stay in the hospital? Will this make me better? Am I even going to get better? The thoughts flooded my mind as I drifted back into the reality of the room I was in. The temperature seemed to rise as I continued to contemplate the news I was receiving. My doctor continued to explain that this was a surgery he was very hopeful about. Very hopeful that this would be the solution and would ultimately keep me from requiring a liver transplant. It was good to hear the hope-filled consultation, but his words of hope seemed to be drowned out by the frustration I was experiencing.

Just like all the tests and procedures before, the date and time was set for my first, major operation. On March 17, 2003 I went under the knife for the first time at 2:35 p.m. Everything went according to plan and I came back out of the surgery without any complications. My doctors seemed optimistic as they were able to accomplish the task they had set out to complete.

However, in spite of high hopes and an optimistic outlook, the operation did not bring about the results we had prayed for. The days following the operation, my doctors continued to monitor the way my health was progressing. But it was not moving the direction we had envisioned. My liver seemed unresponsive and my blood work still was unacceptable. Medications had not solved the problem and now the spenorenal shunt had failed as well.

With this option exhausted that meant only one thing: I was going to need a liver transplant. My doctor explained to me the process of being placed on the national donor list. As I sat there soaking up the bitter news, I remember my head rolling back in frustration. I had become more discouraged than afraid. So much work had gone into avoiding this–a liver transplant. Time, as it was, seemed to stand still for a moment.

I reflected back to when this all began. I didn't foresee myself requiring an operation when my treatments had begun. But one had already come and passed, and now I was looking towards the next. This was another point in the road I hoped I would never see. The news came with a certain amount of fear, of course. But I was more gripped by the discouragement and frustration. The back of my head began to throb and again the temperature in the room seemed to rise. I was ready for this all to be over. My endurance was already waning prior to the last operation. Now I had a whole new obstacle to face.

The blessing of family and friends

After receiving the news, it spread throughout our network of family and friends. My parents had been approached by a family member, and also a close family friend. They both wanted to let my parents know that they had the same blood type as I did and would be willing to be a living donor. How do you acknowledge that type of willingness, let alone thank someone for that kind of selfless generosity? But what was even more humbling than that, without my knowledge, my own sister began going through the testing to see if she could be an acceptable match. My own sister who nearly passed out at the very sight of blood. The same sister who snipped her finger with a pair of scissors in my parents' kitchen and proceeded to faint multiple times.

Knowing what it would require of her to even do the lab work was huge, how could I allow her to put her own life at risk for mine? It is my belief that when siblings experience the passing of a parent together, it creates a uniquely powerful bond. It was the bond that compelled her to take a year off from college, leave her school in Ohio, and come back home to support me and the rest of my family as we walked through this experience together. That same bond is what caused her to selflessly be willing to jeopardize her health for mine.

As we spoke with the doctors about the details surrounding a liver transplant and finding a compatible donor, they soon ruled out the possibility of my sister being a suitable living donor. Due to the fact I was nearly full-grown, I would have required more tissue than she could donate. The liver is an incredible organ. In addition to being your body's filtration system, the liver can also regenerate itself. The liver is composed of two lobes. If one of the lobes is removed the other lobe will re-grow the mass that has been removed. A very unique feature of the liver, but in spite of this fact, the amount of the liver that the recipient receives must be proportional to their body. To be completely honest, a wave of relief washed over me the moment the doctors told us that my sister would not be able to be my living donor. Not that I wasn't thankful: I couldn't bear the thought of seeing my sister go through such an experience for me. This was my battle, not my sister's. An organ is not the type of gift in which you receive and simply say "thanks" or write a nice note in a greeting card. No, I was relieved because I couldn't imagine my sister risking her life for mine.

UNOS, MELD and PELD

Placing a patient on the donor list is a little more complex than what most people seem to think, and the process went a little differently than I had imagined. Whenever I had previously heard about "the list" I simply envisioned them scratching my name down on a clipboard, handing me a number, and telling me to wait for it to be called. You know, the type of waiting you do at the DMV or in a deli.

To my surprise, the national donor waiting list is much more structured than I had ever imagined. It's a lengthy explanation, but UNOS explains the process best for being placed on the national donor list for a liver transplant (the process varies depending on what organ the patient is to receive).

> The United Network for Organ Sharing (UNOS), a non-profit charitable organization, operates the Organ Procurement and Transplantation Network (OPTN) under federal contract. On an ongoing basis, the OPTN/UNOS evaluates new advances and research and adapts these into new policies to best.

> As part of this process, the OPTN/UNOS developed a system for prioritizing candidates waiting for liver transplants based on statistical formulas that are very accurate for predicting who needs a liver transplant most urgently. The MELD (Model for End Stage Liver Disease) is used for candidates age 12 and older and the PELD (Pediatric End Stage Liver Disease Model) is used for patients age 11 and younger.

What is *MELD*? How will it be used?

The Model for End-Stage Liver Disease (MELD) is a numerical scale, ranging from 6 (less ill) to 40 (gravely ill), used for liver transplant candidates age 12 and older. It gives each person a 'score' (number) based on how urgently he or she needs a liver transplant within the next three months. The number is calculated by a formula using three routine lab test results:

Bilirubin, which measures how effectively the liver excretes bile

INR(prothrombin time),which measures the liver's ability to make blood clotting factors

Creatinine, which measures kidney function (Impaired kidney function is often associated with severe liver disease)

The only priority exception to MELD is a category known as Status 1. Status 1 patients have acute (sudden and severe onset) liver failure and a life expectancy of hours to a few days without a transplant. Less than one percent of liver transplant candidates are in this category. All other liver candidates age 12 and older are prioritized by the MELD system.

A patient's score may go up or down over time depending on the status of his or her liver disease. Most candidates will have their MELD score assessed a number of times while they are on the waiting list. This will help ensure that donated livers go to the patients in greatest need at that moment.

What is *PELD*? How does it differ from *MELD*?

Candidates age 11 and younger are placed in categories according to the Pediatric End-stage Liver Disease (PELD) scoring system. Again there is a Status 1 category for highly urgent patients, representing about one percent of those listed.

All other candidates in this age range receive priority through PELD. PELD is similar to MELD but uses some different factors to recognize the specific growth and development needs of children. PELD scores may also range higher or lower than the range of MELD scores. The measures used are as follows:

Bilirubin, which measures how effectively the liver excretes bile

INR (prothrombin time), which measures the liver's ability to make blood clotting factors

Albumin, which measures the liver's ability to maintain nutrition

Growth failure

Whether the child is less than one year old

As with MELD, a patient's score may go up or down over time depending on the status of his or her disease. Most candidates will have their PELD score assessed a number of times while they are on the waiting list. This will help ensure that donated livers go to the patients in greatest need at that moment.

What Led To the *MELD/PELD* System?

Until 2002, patients needing liver transplants were grouped into four medical urgency categories. The categories were based on a scoring system that included some laboratory test results and some symptoms of liver disease.

One concern with using symptoms in scoring was that different doctors might interpret the severity of those symptoms in different ways. In addition, this scoring system could not easily identify which patients had more severe liver disease and were in greater need of a transplant.

Research showed that MELD and PELD accurately predict most liver patients' short-term risk of death without a transplant. The MELD and PELD formulas are simple, objective and verifiable, and yield consistent results whenever the score is calculated.

OPTN/UNOS committees developed the liver policy based on MELD and PELD, with key support from transplant patient/family advocates. It was approved by the OPTN/UNOS Board of Directors in November 2001 and went into effect in February 2002.

How are livers offered through *MELD* and *PELD*?

Livers are offered first to urgent and compatible patients in the donor's local area (often defined as a state or large metropolitan area), then to a larger region of the country (the OPTN/UNOS has 11 allocation regions in the U.S.), then nationwide. Because Status 1 candidates are most medically urgent, each liver is first offered to local Status 1 candidates, then regional Status 1 candidates. The sequence of offers after Status 1 patients depends on the donor's age.

If the donor is younger than 18, after any Status 1s are considered the liver would next be offered to candidates in the region age 11 or younger. The organ would then be considered for local and then regional candidates with a MELD of 15 or higher. Any patients age 12 to 17 would be considered ahead of adult patients.

If the donor is 18 or older, the liver would be offered first to local and regional Status 1 candidates. If not accepted for any of these patients, the liver is then offered to candidates with a MELD/PELD score of 15 or higher, first locally and then regionally.

If the liver is not matched to any candidates with a MELD/PELD of 15 or higher, it may then be considered for local, then regional candidates with a MELD/PELD of 14 or less. Finally the liver would be offered for any compatible candidates nationwide, beginning with Status 1 candidates and then to those with the highest MELD/PELD scores.

How is waiting time counted in the system?

Various studies report that waiting time is a poor indicator of how urgently a patient needs a liver transplant. This is because some patients are listed for a transplant very early in their disease, while others are listed only when they become much sicker.

Under the MELD/PELD system with a wide range of scores, waiting time is not often used to break ties. Waiting time will only determine who comes first when there are two or more patients with the same blood type and the same MELD or PELD score.

If a patient's MELD or PELD score increases over time, only the waiting time at the higher level will count. (For example, if you have waited 40 days with a score of 12, and 5 days with a score of 15, you would only get credit for 5 days of waiting time at the score of 15.) However, if the patient's MELD or PELD score decreases again, he or she would keep the waiting time gained at the higher score. (Using the earlier example, if your score goes from 12 to 15 and back to 12, you would have 45 days of waiting time at the score of 12.) Patients initially listed as a Status 1 also keep their waiting time if their condition improves and they later receive a MELD/PELD score.

Patients with higher MELD/PELD scores will always be considered before those with lower scores, even if some patients with lower scores have waited longer (For example, a patient waiting for one day with a score of 30 will come ahead of a patient with a score of 29, even if the patient with a 29 has waited longer. This is because the patient with a score of 30 has a higher risk of dying without a transplant.).

Dilemmas

After going through the appropriate testing, I originally received a relatively low score. But that was okay, we had started the process and now all we had to do was sit back and wait for my number to be called. Right?

Wrong! We soon discovered an enormous hurdle we would have to leap: working with our insurance company. Until this point, my insurance company had been willing to cover everything at the University of Nebraska Medical Center. But now that I was going to be receiving a liver transplant at the hospital, they decided to no longer cover my care at this hospital. But my parents wouldn't take "no" for an answer.

Now, I say "we" only because it was my liver that was at the center of this struggle with the insurance. It began with a letter to the insurance company requesting that they reconsider their previous decision and allow me to remain in Omaha to receive my liver transplant. At this point it had been nearly two years that I had been visiting the Nebraska Medical Center. My doctors in Omaha had overseen multiple biopsies, my splenorenal shunt, two years of blood work, and several other procedures. It only made sense that I remain in the same hospital with the same doctors who had brought me to this point. Transferring to another hospital at this stage seemed counterintuitive.

The insurance company was unmoved by my parents request to keep my care in Omaha. Instead, they provided us with a list of hospitals they would approve. The only hospital on the list within several hours from home was the very hospital where my father had passed away: not exactly my first choice. But at this point we were not even considering another option. Our church was asked to keep the matter before the Lord. My doctor in Omaha then wrote a letter to our insurance company expressing his concern in transferring my care to a different hospital. His letter, however, was met with the same response my parents had received.

Yet, my parents still were not done. Plan C: my doctor had another one of his physician friends write a letter on my behalf addressing the obvious oversight in transferring a patient's care during such a critical time. The insurance company's response: once again a resounding "no."

My parents continued to plead our case before the insurance company. The next idea was to request the aide of our state senator. There was no way the insurance company could ignore the request of a state senator. But not even at the request of Charles Grassley, the long-standing senator of Iowa, would the insurance company change their mind.

Church congregations prayed, letters were written, but their decision had been made from the beginning. A petition that began with my parents, carried on by my doctors, lifted up in prayer by friends and family, had ended with the final attempted dissuasion by our senator. But I would soon discover that those prayers would be answered in a way we were not anticipating.

[From left to right] My mom, my brother-in-law, Chad, my sister, Nataly, me, and my sister, Sarah just a few moments before flying to St. Louis for my transplant.

CHAPTER 3:
St. Louis

"If you're going through hell, keep going."

-Winston Churchill

It was not quite hell, but it was a labyrinth of frustration. My experience in Omaha had brought answers but left me with an unfulfilled hope. The problem had been discovered, but the sickness had not been remedied. The purpose behind the splenorenal shunt, my first major operation, had proven to be unsuccessful. But no journey is traveled without a few bumps in the road. Sometimes the bumps turn into large roadblocks; blockages so big, they seem to put an end to all forward progress and force an alternate route.

With alternatives exhausted, my doctors resolved to place me on the national organ donor list. Thinking back to when this had all began, I was now fully convinced that *this type of thing, indeed, does happen to me.* The insurance that had, at first, been willing to cover my care was unwilling to work with my doctors through transplantation when I needed it most.

Like a steady rain on a dreary day, the trials didn't seem to let up. But now it began to pour. The date was March 30, 2003; the numbers of the date would have more accurately conveyed the evil that I felt upon my body if multiplied by two: 666. It was one of the darkest moments I experienced during my liver transplant journey and I remember lying on the couch in my parents' basement motionless, restrained by the pain. The symptoms of a failing liver were becoming increasingly evident sending pain throughout every inch of my body. Unlike anything I had ever experienced before, the pain had become so great it rendered me speechless. Fixed in a fetal position, nearly drowning in a pool of pain, my parents rushed me to the hospital as the pain continued to increase. Not until recently did my parents admit they had thought those moments would be the last I would spend in their home as they carried me out the front door.

After we arrived at the Des Moines hospital, I was seated in a wheelchair to wait for my doctor. I sat staring down a hallway as if looking down a corridor leading to my death. I don't remember a lot of the details of this time, I merely remember the pain. It seemed to be on a gradual climb the days leading up to this moment. But on this day it had evolved into an unbearable monster sitting atop my shoulders.

Prior to March 30th, I had been back home and going to school. After the shunt, I had been in the hospital for three months, but since that time I had come back home while continuing to visit my doctors with regular appointments.

Actions speak louder

Motionless I sat and waited for the ambulance that would take me back to Omaha, Nebraska. I was not even sure I would last long enough to see its arrival. For some reason, when I look back on these moments of great pain, my mind seems to darken the mental snap shot. Similar to the way hospitals, some of the most well lit buildings you will ever walk into, are portrayed to be so dimly lit in movies.

As I sat waiting in the stillness of those moments, I remember one of my closest friends, David Smith, coming to visit me before I left. I saw him talking with my mom, but I was in no state of mind to rise to my feet and greet him. I was not even able to say "hi." In that moment he simply placed a baseball cap on my head, squeezed my shoulder, and walked away

37

communicating more encouragement than a thousand words could have provided.

As he walked away I sank lower into my wheelchair both physically and emotionally. My entire being was screaming, "GET ME OUT OF HERE!" I longed for merciful deliverance. I hoped that maybe God would graciously send one of His angels to pick me up and carry me away. The pain was more than I could handle and I wanted to die.

I was rushed back to Omaha to be admitted to the hospital for the next three months. Nearly half of my sophomore year in high school was spent within the walls of this hospital.

Once released from the hospital, I was once again required to wait. Wait for my number to be called. The insurance company had made up their mind and we were forced to choose a new hospital. My doctor walked us through each of the options that our insurance company had provided as acceptable alternatives to my current hospital. Instead of a hospital tour around the country, or a shot in the dark, we asked for my doctor's suggestion. We asked him which hospital he would choose if the decision was his to make.

We considered several options; one of them being in California which is where my mind naturally gravitated. As a teenager, I was more concerned about the view from my hospital room than the convenience of the hospital's location. After much prayer and careful consideration, we decided to select St. Louis Children's Hospital in St. Louis, Missouri. There was one defining factor that set this hospital apart from all the others: it had a strong connection to my current doctor. The doctor over the children's liver transplant team was a close friend of my doctor in Omaha. This little fact went a long way in helping us make our decision.

You couldn't put a price on the peace of mind that came with this new hospital choice, but I sure wasn't going to be seeing any sandy beaches from the window of my hospital room. Looking back I see why my parents didn't leave these decisions entirely up to me. It may have been my health at the center of the decision process, but my preference was based on details such as whether or not I would be able to go to Disneyland while recovering or the proximity of my hospital room to the beach.

St. Louis, Missouri: a long ways from the sandy beaches of California

Four days after Independence Day, my mom and I made the trip to visit my new hospital. It was 2003; just two years away from what I hoped would be my high school graduation. As we stepped off the plane, my mom and I boarded the train that would drop us off a couple blocks away from the hospital. As I filled my lungs with the Missouri air, I was once again struck by an anxious anticipation.

Part of this anticipation was based on the joy of what lay ahead: surgery and recovery. It may sound strange to look forward to surgery with anticipation. However, along with this surgery I knew recovery, and ultimately healing would follow. But the anxiety came from the very same thing: surgery and recovery.

The thought of what lay ahead was both exciting and daunting. A liver transplant was unlike any of the operations or procedures I had experienced until this point. I had come so far but I was not sure how much further I would have to go. As I thought about this surgery, I just wanted to get it over with. Like tearing off a bandage, I wanted the pain of this experience to be done and over with in an instant. I knew this would not be an easy leg of the journey.

Whether a blessing or a curse I can't be sure, but teenagers usually possess a certain amount of perceived invincibility. But at this point I felt a lot more human and a whole lot less super human. I carried two constant reminders of my frail condition. Two drainage bags hung from my stomach at all times to allow fluids to drain from my abdominal region. Not a pretty picture I'll admit, but proof of my failing health.

So many uncertainties crowded my mind and I wanted something to set it at ease. As my mom and I walked into the children's hospital, my easily distracted mind was overtaken by kaleidoscope of colors that covered the interior of the hospital. From my perspective, it looked more like an indoor amusement park than a hospital. I looked down at my feet, the carpet was a vibrant pattern of colorful shapes, to my right I saw a contraption dropping marbles into a wired-maze of loops, and beyond that was something that looked like a life-size hot air balloon. The carnival of colors and happy shapes caused a smile to spread across my face. In fact, all of it made me smile, but it didn't provide the sense of peace I was hoping for. Something that would make me know for certain we had selected the right hospital.

Momentarily after checking in at the front desk, I was greeted by my two transplant coordinators. People have a way of changing the way you look at things. They can either make a place enjoyable or they simply make it dreadful. Lynn and Michelle, my coordinators at Children's, made the experience of a liver transplant as good as it could get from the moment I met them. After recording my vital signs and noting my height, weight, and blood pressure, they provided me with a complete snapshot of what this experience would look like. Together they assumed the role as caretakers of my liver transplant. They were there to keep my healthcare in check. Throughout my transplant if I was doing something I shouldn't be, they quickly informed me. And if I ever neglected to do something I should have done, they were quick to remind me.

I had been introduced to my coordinators, so now it was time to meet my doctor. It felt a little like a scene taken from the *Wizard of Oz*. I had heard so much about this doctor already, but who would be the man who would step out from behind the curtain? What would he look like? What would he sound like? His fame was known far beyond the walls of the hospital.

In my experience with doctors, I have found that there are three types: doctors who should have possibly chosen a different occupation; those who are good at what they do, but lack the interpersonal skills to deal with patients; and then there are doctors who are great at what they do and their patients love them. Dr. Shepherd was the latter. A walking, breathing medical dictionary, there wasn't a question that I could think of that he did not have an immediate answer to. From the moment we met, I enjoyed every conversation we had. As soon as he walked through the door of the exam room he greeted me with a warm smile and a, "Hello, Noah," each syllable sculpted by his native Australian accent. Hailing from Down Under, and by the sound of it, he had not lost any of his natural dialect while living in the United States. He walked over to where I was seated, and sat next to me on the exam table instead of the customary wheelie chair that was provided for the physician. As he stuck his hand out to shake mine, I could not help but think how unusual it was for him to be sitting next to me on the exam table. In all my experience with doctors, I had not seen anything like this. I thought for sure he was breaking some kind of doctor code of conduct. It may have been a small act of hospitality, but it showed me that this doctor could sympathize with me. Looking me in the eyes he asked, "Noah, are you ready to have a liver transplant?"

He took the time to get to know me not only as a patient, but also as a teenager who desperately wanted to get back to life as a high school student. In exchanged he shared who he was outside the walls of the hospital. Beyond a physician he was a family man who enjoyed surfing the waters of Australia every chance he had.

He addressed each of my questions and concerns, and afterwards focused his attention on my mother's maternal apprehension. She is a strong woman, but there was an obvious, lingering concern. My doctor didn't try to side-step the issue, but rather addressed it head on. Turning to my mom he provided us both with the certainty we had been looking for.

"I won't allow what happened to your husband to happen to your son."

This simple statement went miles and miles in placing our minds at ease. It was a thought that had lingered in the back of my mind, "Would the same fate that took my dad away overtake me as well?" I realize that everything happens for a reason and that my father's passing was part of God's plan, but with just a small declaration, my doctor provided God-given peace. As I sat on the exam table, staring down at the brightly colored tile flooring, I was able to breathe a sigh of relief in that moment. I knew we had chosen the right hospital.

The phone call

After the initial appointment, we went back home and continued my pre-transplant care from Iowa. While constantly checking in with my new transplant team, I eagerly waited to receive the call from one of my coordinators letting me know they had a liver for me.

I went back to life as usual. Well, as usual as life can be while waiting for a life-saving organ transplant. And then one night I remember looking at my phone's caller ID as it began to ring. It was the evening of August 24th and I knew exactly why this number was calling, but I wasn't sure how to respond. Not only was this was the call I had been thinking about for so many months now, it was the call we had all been constantly praying for. I had spoken with the psychiatrist about it on multiple occasions, I had prayed for it, but nothing could prepare me for that moment. For a few brief seconds, time nearly stood still as I sat staring at my phone.

At the time I was with a group of friends and I was not sure how I should react. Should I keep my emotions under control? Or do I go lottery-winner-crazy and jump on top of the furniture? I think I displayed an expression somewhere in between as I answered the phone.

Me: "Hello."

Coordinator: "Noah?"

Me: "Yes?"

"Noah, I need you to come to the hospital as soon as you can. We have a liver for you. You're going to have a liver transplant tonight." The call brought the sweetest sounding news. It was the sound of deliverance: the news I was a little concerned might never come. My coordinator's voice was calm, yet direct. I listened as she encouraged me to promptly make my way to the hospital via the pre-planned route they had facilitated.

As I jumped into my car, I have to admit that I quickly realized I had a pretty good excuse for exceeding the speed limit. Hypothetically, I thought how I might respond if an officer were to pull me over while speeding home. *Well, officer, I am on my way to have a liver transplant.* Most likely not an excuse most policemen hear every day.

We had made arrangements with a nonprofit flight group who worked with pilots who offered their services to patients in need of transportation. After meeting my parents at home and picking up the bag I had packed months ago, I found myself standing on the small regional tarmac in Ankeny, Iowa, waiting for the plane to arrive: my transportation that would deliver me to St. Louis for a life-changing event.

Sad movies are not my thing

The smell of the black top filled my nostrils as I stared into the midnight sky anticipating the lights of the plane to appear over the horizon. A few of my family members were there to show their loving support as we anxiously waited together. The night was calm and quiet, except for the distant hum of cars passing by on the interstate a few hundred yards away. It was just my family and myself, no airplane in sight, no other cars in the parking lot. The emotion swelling inside stood in complete contrast to the peace of the quiet, little airport. We spent the time sharing stories that had led me to this point in my journey. And then a flicker of light appeared in the distant sky: like a star burning brighter and brighter as it descended towards the earth.

In eager anticipation, we watched the lights of the small aircraft grow brighter as it neared the landing strip in front of us. My family began to exchange hugs and goodbyes. Filled with hope and joy I said my goodbye. This was a moment of celebratory zeal for life. The next time I would stand in the town I currently stood, I would be a different person; stronger and no longer plagued by a failing liver.

My air ambulance was moments away from taking me to surgery and I couldn't help but be excited. I have never been one for sad movies, and I didn't want this to be one of those sad goodbye moments associated with such movies. To me this was anything but a sad moment! This was a life-changing experience standing in front of me. It meant I would soon get my strength and energy back. I would be able to run, play sports, and be a normal teenager again. No more afternoon naps, yellow eyes, or drainage bags. The runway in front of me lead to new life just beyond.

The final hugs were exchanged and goodbyes spoken as my mom, my sister, and I boarded the plane. Lowering my head, I stepped aboard and lay down on the bed as one of the flight crewmembers began taking my vital signs. My heart began to beat out of my chest as the anticipation grew. It may sound strange, but my concerns about the surgery seemed to dissipate with each passing moment as I got closer to the hospital. I was no longer apprehensive about the operation, but eagerly awaiting as if I was in line at an amusement park.

Landing in St. Louis, our plane was met by an ambulance prepared to take me to the hospital. We arrived at the hospital at 1:30 am on August 25th. For some reason, I had envisioned that I would immediately be rushed into the operating room directly from the ambulance. I assume this idea came from the many dramatic television scenes depicting something similar. Watching a patient casually waiting in a hospital room prior to surgery probably wouldn't make for entertaining TV.

Getting off the ambulance I was carefully assisted into a wheelchair and rolled into the hospital. However, as I entered, I was not rushed anywhere. Instead, everyone seemed to be laid back, taking their sweet time. If I felt like I was in a line to an amusement park before, then apparently the line wasn't moving very fast. After being checked into the hospital, I was taken into a room where I changed, had an IV started, and waited… and waited some more. Every once in a while a nurse would stop by to check on me.

Finally, after what seemed like hours, one of the nurses walked into my room. This time she was there to take me with her. The nurse prepared my bed to be rolled out of the room as I said "goodbye" and gave one last hug to my mom and sister. As she rolled me out of my room and past the clock that hung on the wall, I stared in disbelief. The seemingly endless hours of waiting had only been about one hour. Apparently for patients waiting for a life-saving surgery, hospital time moves at a fraction of the rate it moves outside.

As my nurses guided my bed through the maze of hallways leading to the operating room, I was impressed by the control with which the nurses steered. They came within mere inches of the wall as they turned corners and slid through doorways. Passing under light after light, each one acting as a sequential countdown until we reached the operating room, I lay on my back eagerly awaiting our final destination. Before reaching the doors of the operating room, we made one last stop as the nurse ducked inside a room for a brief moment. "Would you like a warm blanket?" asked the nurse as she reappeared from the laundry room. It did seem a bit strange to be covering up with a warm blanket in the middle of summer: late August to be exact. But this was not my first trip to an operating room and the warm blankets had always been a soothing comfort. This time was no exception. As my bed was pushed through the last set of doors, my face, the only uncovered portion of my body, was hit with the near Arctic temperatures of the operating room.

The vivid lights, the sterile, white walls, the cold, crisp air: it all took me back to my first operation I had gone through several months prior to this.

As my bed was parked next to the operating table, they assisted me off my bed and into place: far more comfortable than I had expected. Movies seem to portray these tables like steel platters. However, one of the nurses explained the painstaking efforts taken to guarantee that the operating table was as comfortable as possible. The table needs to be able to facilitate your body's pressure points for longer than a mere nap. According to the American Liver Foundation, the average liver transplant lasts anywhere from 3 to 12, hours depending on the details of the operation. In general, organ transplants take several hours to complete.

As soon as I was in place, the anesthesiologist, my new best friend (at least for the next several hours), walked forward to introduce himself. Checking my IV, he made sure everything was functioning as it should have been. After making his assessment, he told me that I would feel a warm sensation flowing through my arm as he began the anesthesia. Almost as if someone had spilled a warm drink onto my hand, the sensation began to flow through my hand, up my arm, and into my body.

If any worry or concern remained, it quickly melted away. Looking around the room, my mind relaxed as I took in the sights and smells. The smell of sterile liquids and latex gloves filled the air. As my eyes scanned the room, taking note of the interesting utensils and familiar faces, my breathing became slower. In slow motion I redirected my gaze back to the ceiling as the large lights above compelled my eyes to close. Alone in my thoughts but for a moment, each of the doctors greeted me and reassured me that I was in good hands. Relaxed and moments from sleep, my surgeon stepped forward to let me know they were about to begin.

It seemed like Grand Central Station from what I remember with everyone preparing for this miracle of modern-day medicine. It was the early hours of the morning but everyone was busy working away. In my half–stupor, I felt the energy in the room begin to change as they all moved into place for surgery. The anesthesiologist walked up to me one more time and told me that he would be sending me off to sleep soon. By this point I was more than ready. "I'll see you on the other side," my surgeon said through his paper mask. The anesthesiologist walked over and informed me that he would be placing a mask over my face to help me fall to sleep.

"Count down from ten and you'll be fast asleep," I was told. I smiled as the thought went through my mind. I smiled because one: you never make it past nine. They might as well tell you to count down from two. And two: I was on the operating table to receive my life saving organ transplant. I was moments away from getting my new liver: my new life. A life I was ready to get back. Back to the way things were before this all started.

"Ten… nine…" and I was asleep.

Enjoying the weather with my good
friend, Ronald, while recovering at
the Ronald McDonald House.

CHAPTER 4:
Nick at Nite, Skittles and Recovery

"We are what we believe we are."

-C.S. Lewis

I had already been through my fair share of surgeries to know that waking up from an operation is not the heavenly bliss they portray it to be in the movies. The sharp, fluorescent light seemed to cut through my eyelids as they spontaneously opened up with the anesthesia beginning to wear off. My eyes had opened, but my body, just as quickly, told me to go back to sleep. However, my head started to ache as my senses began to awaken as well. Beginning to recognize voices in the air and seeing the faces around me, I soon realized, through my groggy stupor, that my surgery had been met with at least some amount of success. This certainly was not heaven.

Before I could decide if I should pretend I was still asleep, I heard one of my family members call out, "He's awake!" "Oh, he's awake!" exclaimed my mom in response. My decision had been made for me: there was no more going back to sleep now.

As if my eyelids were connected to a broken pulley system, I fought to keep them open. The details of the room began to take form as my vision slowly came in to focus. Like a fog dissipating with the morning sunrise, I began to more clearly recognize the faces associated with each voice. Everything had a frame of reference: I knew most of the people around me, with the exception of a couple nurses moving about. I knew I was in the hospital and I knew I had just come out of surgery. But was everything okay? *Do I have my new liver?*

I still had not fully awakened. It took a few moments to come to the realization of what was going on around me. The quiet whispers seemed to stop as I looked around the room. *How long had I been asleep?* After the surgery, it didn't feel like I had woken from rest. The nine hours I had been asleep seemed to be a black void. No memories. No dreams. Just darkness. Before I could fully grasp the reality of the moment, my nurse walked back in to ask, "How are you feeling?"

All things considering, I felt pretty good. Nevertheless, still a little dazed and slowly waking up. But one thing I did know was that I was hungry and wanted food: a sure sign that my love for eating hadn't been removed with my old liver. But the more important matter at hand was the outcome of the surgery.

Before I was able to comprehend what was taking place, one of the doctors suddenly appeared at my bedside. Clipboard in hand, he began to explain the details of the surgery. The only detail I could gather was that the surgery had been a success. The rest of his words dissolved into the haze my mind was working to clear. He visited with my family for a few moments and then left.

I took a deep breath, allowing my lungs to fill for the first time out of surgery. All at once, the fog my mind had been sitting in lifted as I awoke to a new reality: I was healed! I had made it through the surgery and I was alive. Although I didn't feel like a million bucks yet, I was headed in the right direction. I had taken the first big step to becoming the stronger version of myself that I had been longing for the past three years. Now, I had my goal in front of me: the road to recovery.

Relax and enjoy the ride

A truth that I realized early on in my recovery is that you should not take life too seriously, but rather enjoy each moment. When my health was taken from me, I began to see each passing moment as a gift from God. Things that had once seemed so important had now lost their value. The stock I once placed in impressing those around me seemed to lose much of its worth. I was more concerned about enjoying each moment of life rather than worrying about the image I was conveying to those around me.

One of the areas affected by this new philosophy was my television preference during breakfast each morning. I'm a creature of habit, and I tend to take comfort in my routine. Every morning throughout my recovery in the hospital, among other things, I ordered my breakfast and after receiving it, watched the same thing on TV. However, my hospital didn't have Sports Center at the time, and I did not enjoy the alternative sports channel option. Instead of subjecting myself to watching something I did not enjoy, I decided I would watch something that would at least make me laugh. So each morning the nurse would find herself taking my vital signs to the lovely sounds of Sponge Bob Squarepants coming from the television on my wall. Somewhere between my first foley catheter and my second enema, I realized that if I was going to make it through this, I had to learn not to take myself too seriously, enjoy each moment, relax, and laugh at the little things.

Playing ball again

Throughout the dog days of recovery there are days filled with good news, days that seem to be filled with news that is not so great, and days that are a combination. One day in particular, I recall it contained very good news. Growing up, sports were a very large part of my life. I played little league baseball until I was twelve, basketball from the time I was eight, soccer throughout junior high, and I had even tried my hand at wrestling. Basketball had been my favorite sport by far. As far as activities went, sports came second only to my love of art. However, after my eighth grade year in junior high school, my doctors told me I could no longer play sports due to my enlarged spleen, which we later discovered was associated with my problematic liver. (To be precise, they told me I could play sports that did not involve contact. Unfortunately, I wasn't a fan of chess).

Before surgery, my doctors had assumed my spleen would go down in size with the replacement of my old liver. And as it turns out, they were correct! After my transplant, one of the first questions I had was whether or not I would be able to play basketball again. I held my breath as I looked at my doctor waiting for his answer. "Yea, I don't see any reason you can't play basketball." I ended up asking all my doctors to make sure I was hearing them correctly. I immediately found a sneaker catalogue and began selecting the pair of shoes I would wear for my return to the basketball court. It was great news, and an amazing blessing indeed. Four years I had been waiting and hoping to hear these words.

That day I was not only cleared to play my favorite sport again, but I was also allowed to go back to participating in my favorite way of staying active. Running was not my cup of tea, but I had learned the importance of physical activity as my health had been hanging in the balance the past several years. In fact, as I write this, I just finished playing a few games of basketball with friends earlier this morning. One jammed finger and a bruised toe later, I came away with a workout I actually enjoyed. After receiving a transplant, I realized how valuable my health is. Your health if a gift, and I implore you to cherish it.

Baby steps

As it is with anything worth fighting for, the fight is not always enjoyable or easy. Those days that contain the not-so-good news can make you want to throw in the towel. Those days may contain unwanted answers to the questions you've been asking, unexpected news you do not want to hear, or those days may come in the form of physical and emotional pain that can plague the earlier days of healing.

The darkest moment during my recovery came several days after my transplant, when my doctors discovered a problem that required another trip back into the operating room for a special procedure. My bile duct was leaking at the place it had been reconnected during surgery. Apparently leaky pipes cause a problem no matter where they are: under your sink or somewhere in your body.

The operation itself was no problem. Everything went according to plan: the bile duct was reconnected the way it needed to be and was immediately working properly. But it was what happened after the operation. I was given the proper amount of anesthetic to cover any discomfort during the operation, but it ended up being a more complex procedure than they had anticipated. As a result, my body came out of the operation under a greater amount of pain. For the next 48 hours, my doctors and nurses tried to play catch-up with my pain management.

Prior to this operation, I'd often heard people describe excruciating pain as though they had been stabbed. I had always thought this assessment was a little dramatic. *There is no way someone could fathom the type of pain a stab wound would cause unless they have actually been stabbed,* I concluded. That was until I experienced the kind of agony I went through during the next two days. The painful sensation could only be compared to that of a stab wound. I don't say that because I've personally gone through such an experience of being stabbed, but because there is no other pain I could imagine comparing it to.

Pain, emotional hurt, psychological fatigue, or frustration: you may consider them hurdles, battles, or detours on a road to recovery. However you define them, my journey was marked with a few obstacles along the way. As the Scottish politician, Walter Elliot once said, "Perseverance is not a long race; it is many short races one after the other." The times I was most frustrated were the times I became impatient with myself. I often found myself looking too far down the road. Seeing the end in the distance, I wanted to be able to jump the length of road in between the finish and where I currently stood.

In times of pain, I tried to focus on reaching the end of that painful moment or making it until the next dose would come; when I was doing my breathing exercises, I couldn't allow myself to become frustrated by how weak my lungs had become, but rather focused on *that* particular breathing exercise to make it through. I forced myself to look at the snap shots of my recovery instead of the thread of pictures as a whole. I had greater success when I sought to succeed in each moment rather than trying to conquer the mountain with one leap.

Conquering the hurdles of recovery often required many baby steps. Plenty of times I tried to jump the mountain in one leap, and this usually resulted in me falling on my face or finding myself very discouraged. Even my eating was a gradual process after transplant. I couldn't start out consuming pizza and cheeseburgers the moment I came out of surgery (although I may have been dreaming about it). The first thing I was allowed to place in my mouth after surgery was a strange minty-flavored sponge that I could chew on. And then I graduated to ice chips, then a Popsicle, then Jell-O, and then, on August 30th, 2003, I was allowed to eat *solid foods!* Accepting progress in small step-by-step quantities was never easy, but it was often necessary. However, not all of my recovery was measured in baby steps and small doses. Eventually, my healing began to progress by large jumps and great strides.

"There will be a lot of three steps forward and two steps back," says Dr. Jeffrey Lowell, the doctor who performed my transplant at St. Louis Children's Hospital. Dr. Lowell named the recovery process as the hardest thing to communicate to would-be transplant patients. "People expect miraculous transformations, but it took years for you to get this sick and it may take a few months to recover," he further explains. I was told from the beginning my recovery process wouldn't look the same as every other patient, but it would require patience just the same.

The good news was often mingled with the not-so-good. Sometimes the not-so-good news even took the wind from my sails. But it was never a reason to give up. Prior to my transplant, the doctors had informed me that my type 1 autoimmune hepatitis could manifest itself again in the new liver. It was something we hoped we would not have to face, but we knew it was a possibility. However, my one-year check-up, after surgery, brought that exact news. My doctors explained to me that the disease was, in fact, back in the new liver. They had been watching for it, and therefore were able to treat it. Throughout my experience I developed a tough skin to such news. I accepted the news with a determination to press on. However, as my mom and I sat on the edge of my hospital bed, I could see her hope fall to the floor. My mother is one of the strongest individuals I know, but there is something about a parent seeing their child suffer that can render them powerless. This wasn't a scratch on my knee that she could bandage.

In that moment I realized I had a duty. A man that I have come to greatly respect over the years, in fact, the man who was involved in delivering this news, Dr. Ross Shepherd, once shared a piece of advice with me. He said that as the patient going through these trying times, you must be willing to support your family as well. They are constantly there to uphold you, encourage you, and help you carry on. However, as a patient, I was not the only one going through this: I was going through this together with my family. In that moment, I quickly reassured my mom that I was okay. It was simply another detail in God's great big plan for my life.

Hanging out with Ronald McDonald

I was blessed by some extraordinary people throughout my transplant. There were the obvious blessings such as family, close friends, and my doctors, but there was an endless list of people who didn't fall into one of those categories. And while it wasn't one particular person, I had the privilege of being a part of the Ronald McDonald House during my recovery in St. Louis.

When looking at the grand equation that makes up a transplant, lodging is often overlooked. You find a hospital that is right for you, work with the transplant team, and then you have the surgery, but where you'll stay during recovery is often an overlooked detail. As a seventeen year old, this was a detail that never even crossed my mind. But one thing you must realize is that if you're not from the same state, or even the same city as your hospital, it can create a real problem.

When I was released from the hospital after my transplant, I was required to come back to the hospital for daily appointments. Needless to say, going back home to Iowa during my first month out of transplant was not an option.

An out of town patient who cannot go home each night is left with limited options. Without family in town to stay with, our options were scarce. When left to these constraints, what does a patient in this situation do? We were fortunate enough to be blessed by the Ronald McDonald House of St. Louis, Missouri. I had always been a big fan of their fries, but I soon became an even bigger fan of their charitable organization.

Other than having to be readmitted into the hospital for a few days, I spent the next 30 days recovering in this house. It almost felt like staying with a grandmother for a month. The refrigerator was always full and satisfied my every craving; the cupboards completely stocked; a hot meal was served each night; but my favorite part of the house was the brown leather couch situated perfectly in front of the television.

My appetite during the first days out of transplant was not what it is today. Now that I think about it, I do not recall the last time someone told me I needed to eat more. However, during moments of forceful eating I wondered if my appetite would ever come back (for your information, it did come back…and probably even bigger than before).

Throughout those early days of my suppressed appetite I was encouraged to eat whatever and whenever. It may not have helped a whole lot with packing on the pounds or even adding to my daily caloric intake, but my snack of choice was often Skittles. I even had a special water bottle with a secret compartment at the bottom to store my candy stash. After dinner each night, I found my way to the living room, and dropped myself into the inviting arms of the big, brown leather couch. I followed a strict routine of Nick at Nite therapy my first thirty days out of transplant. The television in front of me, the couch beneath me, Skittles in one hand, and a tall bottle of water in the other. This was one of the little things I looked forward to each day. And not a night was missed during that first month.

CHAPTER 5:
Coming Home

"The world breaks everyone, and afterward,
some are strong at the broken places."

-Ernest Hemingway

If I'm being honest, the idea of going home sometimes felt like an unattainable reality. It felt like the door to going home would open for a moment and would snap shut the instant I began to walk through. It had been four years since this journey had begun that led me to St. Louis. Going back home, more than five hours away, seemed too good to be true. I was certain I would experience another set-back or have an unsatisfactory test result that would prevent me from going home for at least a while longer.

In the hospital, whenever I had a fever it was an indication of something more. It didn't mean I simply had the flu, which is what I usually associated with fevers. It meant something more was brewing under the surface. It indicated there was an infection somewhere. With daily appointments, my doctors were able to keep a close eye on the situation, but an infection was a serious problem that had to be solved. Even the smallest problem, when left unchecked turns into a great crisis.

My first two weeks out of the hospital were marked by a consistent fever. Spiking in the evening and subsiding by morning, I hoped for the best, but feared the inventible: that the fever would land me back in the hospital.

As the days carried on, the infection persisted and my fever would return each night. The little fever that could was relentless and wouldn't let up. Each morning I would wake up feeling great, but with each night, the fever would return.

That hope turned into despair when my doctor ordered that I be readmitted into the hospital. I felt as if I had taken one step forward with my hospital discharge, only to take two steps backwards after being readmitted. I could try to sugar coat it and say "it's all part of the recovery process," but ultimately, this turn of events was deeply discouraging. I had just been released from the hospital, going back was the last thing I wanted to do.

This was my Everest that I had been climbing the past four years. I wasn't sure how far I was from the top or exactly how long it would take me to climb this mountain when I began. But at this point, the top of my mountain could not be far. I knew that it was almost in view from where I stood.

Although I had very little control over the fever my body was battling I began to kick myself for the negative progress I was experiencing. All too recent memories came flooding back as testing and procedures began again in order to conquer the infection that had embedded itself within my body.

It would be inaccurate to say this never happens. After living in such a controlled environment in the hospital, it is certain there will be a surprise or two during the first week out. A practice in the discipline of mind over matter: it was imperative that I remain focused on my recovery. Two step backwards was what it took for my body to side step an even larger hurdle. The recovery process can be just as much mental as it is physical. As my body was recovering physically my mind had to remain strong in order to facilitate my body's progress.

Mental toughness

Physically I was taking my medications, getting rest, hydrating my body, and doing everything else the doctor demanded in order to make a complete recovery. But as my doctors repaired my physical condition, it was imperative that I maintain my mental strength. Throughout the healing process, my mind had to remain strong even while my body was weak.

Like a rolling tide, my mental endurance would rise and fall. That is why I found it so important to keep family and friends close, especially throughout this time. During my recovery, it was mandatory that I have friends and family close to me that I could talk with, cry with, and laugh with. I needed someone with whom I could share thoughts, feelings, and emotions: many of which I had never experienced before. When someone says, "Oh, he is a fighter. He'll make it through." they're not referring to physical strength. It's mental and emotional toughness they're referring to.

For me, one of the greatest methods of maintaining my mental toughness was to add a future event to my calendar. Just as it was important to have activities throughout the day to disrupt the monotony, it was also important to have future events to look forward to.

Every red-blooded, teenage, American boy has one thing in common: they cannot wait for their first car. The sense of pride that comes with your first set of car keys is unmistakable. They represent freedom, independence–the first step toward manhood. At least it felt that way for me.

From age sixteen to seventeen I had spent a lot of my time in and out of the hospital. The purchase of my first car was relegated to a distant future event. Being restrained to a hospital bed usually prevents a kid from purchasing a car. That is, unless you are related to my brother. With his help, I was able to purchase my first car from my hospital bed, five hours from home.

To be more accurate, my first automobile was a truck. A 1997 white Chevrolet S-10 pickup truck. I say "pickup truck" lightly because it was light on the *truck* part. Not exactly what you think of when you see a 4X4 commercial on TV. In these commercials you'll hear a rough, masculine voice describing each feature as you watch the truck climb over large boulders while pulling a trailer the size of a house. My truck wasn't featured in any such advertisement. In high school when one of the guys asked if someone had a truck to borrow, I was never quick to lend my hand. Not that I wasn't proud of my truck, I just knew what they had in mind and my truck didn't necessarily fit that description. But at sixteen, I could have been driving Fred Flintstone's car and been happy.

After emailing me pictures and talking numbers, we settled on a price. I could not believe it. I had bought my first car and I was still in the hospital! But now I had to wait at least a whole month before I would even see the car? It would be pure torture, but definitely something to look forward to.

A few days later my brother gave me the surprise of a lifetime. He and my sister-in-law drove my little truck all the way to St. Louis just so I could see it. By this time I was out of the hospital again, but still staying in St. Louis. As soon as they pulled up I jumped from the couch, bolted through the door, with every intention of taking my new pride and joy for a drive!

Except that there was one minor problem. It had a manual transmission and I had never driven a manual. For all of you who have had the opportunity to learn to drive a manual transmission, you know it takes a little time to get the hang of it. I was not about to make my first attempt on a busy St. Louis street.

So instead of driving my truck, I was content to enjoy the passenger seat while my brother was in St. Louis. We took it to go for dinner later that night. Great idea! More time with my truck. However, that trip to the restaurant is one I will never forget. A Chevrolet S-10 truck fills up quickly when it only has two bucket seats and you have four people riding together. But thankfully I weighed a few pounds less in those days of recovery. Any more weight loss and I nearly could have fit in the glove box.

Home

The arrival and departure of my truck made the light at the end of the tunnel that much brighter. Now I could see the end.

A few days after my brother went back home with my truck, I was sitting on the edge of the doctor's exam table, waiting where I had found myself so many times before. There was the phrase that I wanted to hear my doctor tell me, and the one I assumed I would hear. "Let's run some more tests, see how you do tonight, and see you back in here in the morning," or something along those lines.

But instead I heard, "You're free to go home, Noah." My doctor said it so casually I wasn't sure I heard him right. *Home, home? As in, back to Iowa, home?* He most likely meant I was free to leave the premises of the hospital to go back to the Ronald McDonald House for the night… *right?* But as I looked at my doctor a moment longer, he was clearly referring to home… as in my house back in Des Moines, Iowa.

To be honest, the thought of going back home was a little scary at first. These were the words I had been waiting for now more than two and a half months. But now that I had heard them I wasn't so sure. *Am I ready to go back home? Am I prepared? Am I strong enough? Do I know how to take care of myself? My doctor will be five hours away…*

It seemed so anticlimactic. I don't know what I expected from this moment. Maybe a hospital discharge ceremony; some fanfare to send me back out into the real world; or possibly a post-transplant assessment to see if I was ready to handle myself outside of the hospital now that I would be more than a few blocks away.

Walking through the doors to leave the examination room that day, an overwhelming sense of freedom washed over me. It was as if I was taking the first steps into a new voyage–like a bird that has discovered the cage door is open. It was so exciting… but also a little scary at the same time. There was so much I needed to remember. Rules to follow. I had been without my nurse's call button for a few weeks, but now I could only reach my doctors and coordinators by phone. No longer would I be living down the street from their office.

But then the second wave of reality struck me: *I'm actually going home!*

An unmistakable smile permanently formed across my face. Any anxiety about going home was replaced by the idea of seeing all my family again;

seeing my friends again; being able to hang out in my own room; and being able to sleep in my *own* bed! Free at last! Thank God Almighty!

A little more than two months after my surgery I was back home. From where I stood, it felt like a lifetime separated the two. I was experiencing a moment I had thought about and even meditated on so many times over the past two months. The thought of getting to come home had been the fuel that carried me through so many trying times over the past eight weeks.

But this event was about more than just getting to leave the hospital and come home. I had been healed. Taking in the sights and sounds of home, I walked down the stairs that led to my bedroom. Opening the door, I stared into the room, left untouched, just as it was two months earlier when I had run through that same door to catch my plane. The desk stool I had tripped over was still in the same, inconvenient location. The only difference in the room was the blanket of get-well cards that now covered my bed.

Coming home from the hospital this time around was much different than the previous time I had been discharged from a hospital. The last time I was sent home with a great, daunting course still in front of me. But now my transplant was behind me and I was ready to move on to what life had in store for me.

Still standing on the threshold of my bedroom door, I was poised to step into the next chapter of my life. Coming through trials and tribulations had provided a fresh perspective on my life. Mentally and spiritually I was refreshed. Physically, I was bruised and battle worn, but my mind and my will had been strengthened. Now, more than ever before, I was ready to take on whatever life had in store.

Something that can only be explained by the experience itself, my transplant had relieved me of many fetters, which before had held me fast. Although I was still sapped of energy, physically much weaker than I had been, I felt lighter: relieved of the fear that had previously gripped me.

The next chapter in my life would lead me back to school just a few days later. I rejoined the rest of my class to finish the remainder of my eleventh grade year. Typically I was not a fan of school, but I had never been happier to be back in class.

Patience

On the outside, I was a skeleton of what I was before my surgery: two-thirds of the weight I was when I had begun this journey. But I was so much more ready for what lay ahead of me. I was stronger mentally, and on my way to becoming a physically stronger, healthier version of myself.

I was so excited about life! I was home from the hospital and I now had a healthy liver filtering everything inside of me, but I still had to be patient with myself. It was easy for my mind to get ahead of my body the first couple months after arriving home. At times I would forget about everything my body had gone through and expect my strength and energy to be at the same level it was three years earlier.

I was no longer in the hospital and I was back to a mostly normal schedule. But my body could not quite keep up with what my mind expected of it. Taking afternoon naps was a thing of the past. I did that when I was sick. But now that I had gone through a transplant I felt as though naps should remain a thing of the past and no longer required. My energy did come back, but it took some time. The length of time is different for each patient, but it was longer than I thought was appropriate for myself. I did not want to "take it easy" as my doctors suggested. I had been taking it easy the past two months in a hospital.

Getting back to life

Growing up in Iowa, I was raised to be a diehard, black and gold bleeding, University of Iowa, Hawkeye fan: even during several seasons when there wasn't much to cheer for. In spite of the often unbalanced score displayed above or the unfavorable record, for me, there is nowhere quite like Kinnick

Stadium on a cool, fall day. Located in Iowa City, Iowa, the stadium is home to the University of Iowa Hawkeye football team.

My first football game after getting out of the hospital: I could not wait to drink it all in. Watching my favorite football team would be even more special this time than it had been in the years past. As a family we had a tradition of attending at least one game together each season. And before each game we would attend a pre-game barbecue with my uncle on the lawn of the University's law school.

The crisp air in my lungs, colors of fall splashed across the wooded skyline, and all-American football spirit in the air. I loved every sight, smell, and sound about the experience.

There was only one problem with this tradition: parking. The football stadium doesn't have an abundance of parking spots. The pay-to-park areas make the stadium's overpriced hotdogs look like a bargain and the one parking ramp is usually filled before sunrise. This led us to another family tradition: parking in our undiscovered parking lot. The reason it was still undiscovered so many years after we had discovered this gem was due to the fact it was miles from the stadium.

Walking from a parking lot nearly bordering the next county was not a problem in years prior to this. In fact, I had usually enjoyed the hike. In previous years it allowed our excitement for the game to build as we made our way to the stadium. But this year wasn't the same. Excited as I was to see a football game, I was less than excited about the distance between the location of the game and the secret lot. I would like to say I climbed the great number of stairs to the location of the pre-game barbecue with arms raised high in Rocky-like triumph. But I felt more like Frodo Baggins on my way to Mordor in *The Lord of The Rings*. Quite literally, I was learning to conquer my goal of reaching the destination one step at a time. A lesson I would continue to learn on my road to recovery.

Approaching the stadium, I first began to hear the band inside, and then the stadium itself began to rise above the trees. Never had walking to the football stadium seemed like such an epic accomplishment.

It was times like these I forced myself to take each deliberate step. Their combined sequence eventually led me to my destination. Success doesn't come without a fight whether it's as simple as walking to a football game or as complex as reaching a full recovery after major surgery. For several months, now, my days had revolved around attaining goals. As soon as I could see the stadium, I couldn't take my eyes off it.

The journey ahead

It required I stop to catch my breath a couple more times than I would have liked to admit, but in the end, I made it to the football stadium.

It's been over ten years since my transplant and that infamous hike to the stadium. I have a beautiful wife, a wonderful little girl, and we're anxiously awaiting the arrival of our newest addition to our family this summer.

I overcame the mountain I encountered in the Midwest, but mental, emotional, and physical challenges never stop in life. When I pause to reflect on each of the obstacles I've been allowed to overcome, I'm reminded of a quote by the Lebanese poet, Khalil Gibran. In regards to the trials of life he once said, "Out of suffering have emerged the strongest souls; the most massive characters are seared with scars." In my journey, I discovered suffering and trials to be a necessary building block in life. After reaching the summit of my transplant, I embraced the beautiful view from the top. However, unlike a mountain climber, I didn't want to go back down. My journey prepared me to keep going higher.

PART 2

My Guide On Transplant Success

Throughout my transplant, I uncovered several insights along the way that made my experience more pleasant and my journey more successful. Some of the things I discovered I wished I had learned earlier in order to avert needless headaches and frustrations. But it is my hope that as I offer these suggestions you will be able to avoid some of these headaches and frustrations. I want to keep you from some of the mistakes I made and offer you some of the wisdom and secrets I discovered along the way.

The advice I offer are simply suggestions. Always be sure to check everything with your doctor and coordinator before moving forward.

Pre-Transplant

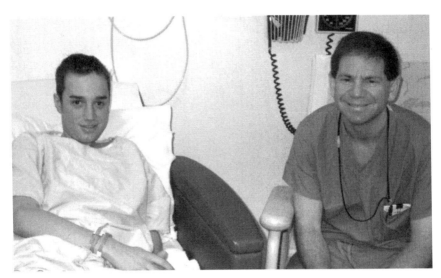

Spending time with my surgeon, Dr. Lowell.

CHAPTER 1:

Your Parents Know what They're Talking About and Your Doctors Do too: Listen to Your Doctor's Advice

> *"I am not a product of my circumstances.*
> *I am a product of my decisions."*
>
> *-Stephen Covey*

I have discovered at each stage in life, hindsight is always 20/20. I've looked back on many of my past decisions and questioned why the younger me made the decision I did. Throughout my teenage and college years in particular, it required me learning some hard lessons on my own. I often felt as though I needed to test the waters even though I had previously been warned by my parents, teachers, or leaders about many of the experiences I would encounter. It was because they had already been down the road I was on (a road that maybe looked a little different back then, but the same road for the most part) and they knew what obstacles lay ahead. They warned me in order to keep me from unneeded pain, not to create displeasure in my life.

When I look back on my transplant experience, the same concept of preventive direction applies to my doctors, nurses, and coordinators. Just as my parents made me do my homework so that I would get good grades in order to go to college and a curfew to protect me, the exercises, recommendations, and medicines my doctors prescribed were for my own good. Your doctors, nurses, and coordinators have walked this road with many patients before you. They know what lies ahead. They will advise you to stick to a course for a reason. Not to make your life more difficult, but rather they know what to expect. They will advise a track that will lead you to the best outcome. And this applies to what your doctors and nurses are telling you both before your transplant and what they are telling you after your transplant. Just because something may not seem important to you, doesn't mean that it's not significant to the process.

I can still remember the few days after my transplant when all I could think about was food. There were moments that if I closed my eyes I would literally dream about cheeseburgers. But my diet during those first days out of surgery was predominantly an all-liquid diet. It began with the mint-flavored sponges and progressed toward Jell-O cups. The sponges hardly quenched my thirst and were, by no means, a substitute for a cheeseburger. They were similar to sucking the moisture out of your toothbrush after you have rinsed it off. After the minty sponges, I was able to move to popsicles, and then I proceeded to Jell-O cups. I have never eaten so much Jell-O in my life. I remember someone saying, "Wow, Noah must really like Jell-O!" I thought to myself, "I've never liked Jell-O, but right now it might as well be a steak dinner!"

As soon as the liquid and semi-liquid diet days were behind me, and before the phase when I struggled with eating, for a time, all I could think about was food. I immediately began eating my way through my grocery list of cravings. And as you can tell by now, a juicy cheeseburger was atop that list, followed by a milk shake, cotton candy, and jumbo-sized dill pickles. But the appetite did not last long. Unfortunately, as I previously mentioned, there was a time shortly after transplant when eating was a chore. Despite being in a hospital with an almost exhaustive menu and a mom who would jump at any verbalized craving, there were weeks when I could not even stomach the thought of food. There were times my mom, nurses, and doctors almost had to force food down my throat.

It stands to reason that while you are inactively lying in bed for weeks on end, there may be periods of time you are not going to be able to work up much of an appetite. In addition to inactivity, certain medications can have an appetite suppressing affect.

But your doctors are not demanding that you eat because they envy your shrinking waistline. An appropriate caloric intake is for your own good. Even though you do not feel hungry, your body needs food. It becomes even more crucial as they start to take you completely off the intravenous proteins (if you are on them). Even though you may have a suppressed appetite and you do not feel hungry, you still need to eat. Your medications and steroids become the ammo by which your body fights this battle of healing and recovery, but your body needs the fuel in order to do so.

Your appetite will return. In the meantime, find a way to consume the number of calories your transplant team has given. You may have to get creative. I hesitate offering too many recommendations because your diet can be a sensitive topic. This is a conversation for you and your dietitian. An open dialogue with your dietitian is essential if eating becomes an issue. You aren't the first transplant patient to struggle with eating.

In addition to requiring food for strength, it is also very important that your bowels become active again. Your intestines have been sitting nearly dormant the past several days and to keep you from further constipation (you will get used to discussing these types of topics... don't worry), it is imperative that everything starts "moving again" as I often heard my nurses and doctors refer to it.

We all become quite comfortable talking about our bowls in the hospital (some more than others). Candor isn't spared during recovery. In reaction to your medications, you may experience minor cases of constipation from time to time, and your doctors and nurses will know what to do with each case, but your calorie consumption can play a large role in preventing this. Take advantage of these things that are within your control.

If your doctor has you on dietary restrictions then these are the nutritional guidelines you need to follow. But if your doctor simply wants you to start consuming calories, then maybe you should try something besides what the hospital menu provides if it doesn't sound appetizing. Allow some creative flexibility into your meal planning throughout the week. If it helps, stray away from the four or five items you get to choose from the hospital menu for each meal if it has been approved by your dietician. There are times that you simply need to get enough calories in your body whether that comes by a diet of pizza and milkshakes or burgers and French fries (just make sure you are getting some nutritional value into your diet at some point). These are the times when you listen to *what* you are craving and *when* you are craving it. There were days when a family member or a friend would bring me my favorite snacks or food from a restaurant, and that alone would prove to be such a relief.

I was fortunate enough to have my liver transplant in a hospital that had a Dairy Queen that remained open most hours of the day. Some nights I would get a craving for a chocolate milkshake at 11:30 and I always made sure to let my nurse know. They catered to my every craving, no matter what time of the day or night the cravings occurred.

In every situation, make sure you are following the dietary guidelines according to what your doctors and nutritional counselors have set for you. In the case that you are following a more rigid diet do not be afraid to ask for all your options. You may have more options than you know of and your dietician may be able to be more flexible or more creative with your menu. This may be the only time that you have a whole team of professionals watching your diet and considering what is best for you, so take advantage of it.

The same rules apply to hydration. You may find that acquiring a thirst may not come naturally when you are not able to get out of bed to go for a walk, let alone be active in the least bit. But when your nurses are keeping a log of the number of ounces you consume in a day, you will find that sometimes you have to force yourself to drink something. As your doctors and nurses will inform you, staying hydrated is essential to your overall health and to protecting your kidneys. The amount of medications you take can be hard on your kidneys if you aren't consuming the proper amount of fluids. You can protect your organs by drinking the appropriate amount of fluids each day.

It always helped me to understand things in my own way as to why things were important and should be obeyed. Mental pictures have always helped me get a better grasp of a subject. So I offer you the following illustration in regards to the importance of fluid consumption. Think of your medications as boulders working their way through a narrow river. A little stream cannot allow rocks to roll down the riverbed if they are too large. If left unchecked, these large boulders will stop up the river and make a complete mess of it. Likewise, it is difficult for such large "boulders" to pass through your kidneys. The water, and different beverages you consume allow these medications to pass through your kidneys in a more manageable state without damaging them. You will feel a positive difference in the way in which you feel if you remain hydrated.

Whenever possible, I found it beneficial when I was able to incorporate the tasks my doctor would give me into my daily routine. I found this made the exercises easier to accomplish. Specifically when it came to drinking enough fluids each day, a practice that I found to be helpful was to take five big drinks during every commercial of the TV show that I was watching throughout the day. Placing the act of drinking into a schedule will force you to drink, even in times when you are not thirsty and do not feel like drinking a glass of water. You can apply this practice to many different activities. Maybe when reading, you can take a drink when you come to the bottom of a page. Or maybe at the end of every chapter in case you're a faster reader than I am. The idea of this practice is to associate taking a drink with something that follows a regular interval and will remind you to take that next drink. Otherwise, you simply leave a big glass of water next to your bed in hopes that you will get thirsty enough at some point in the day and want to drink it. Or you have the option to chug large amounts of water all at once. With either of these options, you'll end up dreading the thought of drinking the water and keep putting it off.

Whatever pattern you choose to follow, I encourage you to choose something that follows a consistent pattern. Don't choose to follow something that happens so often that you get annoyed of constantly taking drinks, but also avoid something that occurs so infrequently that you're unable to consume enough water throughout the day. Remind yourself that keeping your body well hydrated is helping your body recover more quickly.

You need to make sure that you are eating and drinking so that, ultimately, your body has the strength to heal.

CHAPTER 2:
What to Do While You're Waiting

"Courage is found in unlikely places."

-J.R.R. Tolkien

Depending on whether you're on the national donor list or will have a living donor will greatly influence your pre-transplant experience. If you find yourself in the place I was in, and you are placed on the list, you will feel like you have won the lottery when you get that call informing you that they have an organ for you. It's a call you definitely don't want to miss. While you wait you must continue to live life, but always make sure you are within your phone's service area. However, don't allow this to be a time of nervous anticipation. Just as my doctors watched my health with a watchful eye, your doctor will be doing the same with you. The medical field has come a long way, and the national donor list works well.

The list

There is a lot of confusion in regards to the national donor list and how patients are "scored" on it. Some people have speculated that a person with more money or celebrity status or the right connections can get moved up higher on the list, closer to the front of the line. However none of these rumors are true.

To get a better sense of how the list operates, see the section titled "UNOS, MELD and PELD" within chapter 2 for further explanation.

Recommendations

Before you get to the point of receiving the call, there are a few things to consider. These are a few recommendations that I followed before being placed on the list and then after I was placed on the list, but still awaiting for the call.

#1: Be comfortable with your hospital

If you have an option of the hospital at which you will be having your operation, make sure you are making an informed decision. Yes, there are many fine hospitals throughout the country, but you want to make sure it is a hospital you feel comfortable with. Before you go any further in your decision process, consult with the Organ Procurement and Transplant Network (OPTN) website. Dr. Shepherd suggests a few statistics to review when choosing a hospital: waiting list mortality, one and three year patients, and graft survival.

If you can, go visit the hospital before you make your decision. You can visit the U.S. Department of Health & Humans Services' organ donor website (www.organdonor.gov) in order to find a list of transplant hospitals.

Your insurance may play a role in deciding what hospital and doctor you choose. This isn't necessarily a bad thing and actually might prove to make a daunting list of hospitals more manageable when reviewing potential transplant facilities. It is a big choice to make, but I arrived at my decision based on the guidance of my previous doctor. However you choose to make this decision, make sure you've selected a hospital and a doctor that you are comfortable with.

Along with being comfortable with the hospital, you also need to make sure that this hospital is feasible to get to from where you live. Depending upon your arrangements, will you be able to get to this hospital in time once you receive the call? According to Barnes Jewish Hospital, you either need to be able to drive to the hospital or make the appropriate arrangements to be able to get to the hospital within six hours of receiving the call. And then beyond your transplant, will you be able to make it back to this hospital as often as your doctors expect? You will establish a close, long lasting relationship with these people and you want to make sure that you are able to, realistically, make it back as often as you need. This is especially important within the first few months after your transplant. If your hospital is not within driving distance, you may be able to find a transportation group who would help you get to the hospital more efficiently. You can ask your coordinator for recommendations on how to go about contacting such groups. This may be something your coordinator prefers to handle.

#2: Maintain your health and good nutrition

It's important you maintain your health during this time of waiting. Depending upon how well you feel as you wait, you should try to remain active. In addition to having a strong support network, Dr. Jeffrey Lowell of St. Louis Children's Hospital strongly recommends that patients maintain their nutrition and physical strength through exercise while waiting on the donor list. This will help with your outlook on life and will also assist in your recovery after the transplant.

This does not mean that you need to try to run a marathon while you are on the waiting list. Active may be relative to what you've considered active up to this point. Most likely you won't be able to keep up with the pace your life was moving at before your illness. Making it through the day was a chore in itself at times. But simple things that keep you active such as going for walks or playing a sport you enjoy can be very beneficial. Do what your body allows you to do. The extent to how far you can push your body during this time will be different for everyone. I was fortunate enough to be able to remain active during the months I was on the waiting list. Basketball, running, and a regular fitness routine helped me to maintain as much of my body's strength as I could.

While you focus on maintaining your health during pre-transplant, it is also important to try and maintain some sense of normalcy in your day-to-day life. Try to remain on somewhat of a normal schedule. It is still important to remain active and keep your sanity even though you may not have your usual amount of energy. You may have to schedule a nap at some point in your day, but do not allow yourself to be pulled away from your personal life. If you are in school, try, as often as you can, to make it to class. Spend time with your friends and family. And don't neglect your hobbies and other activities you enjoy as much as possible.

Preserving both your physical and mental strength is essential as you look forward to receiving your transplant, as this will prepare you for this huge step you are about to take. In regards to preparing for this life event, Dr. Shepherd says, "Be prepared and think positive, but be realistic–this means learning about transplants and thinking through all the options and possible outcomes. Prepare like [you are] going into training. This will be one of the biggest events in your life." The more proactive you are in your transplant care, the better. Questions will arise during your pre-transplant care. These are questions you should be asking of your transplant team. You will be more prepared and better equipped if you know about the transplant you will be going through.

It's also very important that you watch what you eat. I neglected my diet, for a time, before receiving my transplant and I saw the adverse effects it had on my body. My doctor was appalled at my lab results during one of my weekly appointments. Sadly, it wasn't just the blood work numbers that looked bad, but my blood and fluids themselves were starting to look bad. I've often heard parents jokingly say, "If you eat any more of that, you're going to turn into it." Well, if that was possible, I was probably one drive-thru order away from it.

When I began to disregard my health it quickly became apparent to my doctors. However, you shouldn't wait for your doctors to correct your nutritional habits. Proactively take responsibility for what you put into your body on a daily basis. Your body needs all the help it can get from your food throughout this time.

#3: Maintain your support group

Your physical health must remain extremely high in priority, but you cannot afford to overlook your emotional and mental health as well in this time and all throughout your transplant journey. Maintaining a strong support group around you is an essential key to your successful transplant journey. I cannot say enough about how much of a blessing my family, close friends, church family, and classmates were to me through this time, and even still are today. There will be days when you need someone to lean on. There will be days when the encouraging word of a friend is what keeps you going. There are certain encouraging notes, letters, and verses that I received while in the hospital that I am still reading more than ten years later. When you are going through your day, it is an incredibly helpful thought to know you are in the minds of others.

Arriving at the hospital: breathe, relax and repeat

When you first arrive at the hospital for your transplant there is one very important, non-negotiable rule to remember: *relax*. You are in the hands of very capable professionals, you've had some time to get to know these people by now, and they want to see you succeed in this experience. And if that does not help you relax, you can take comfort in the numbers. According to the United Network for Organ Sharing (UNOS), there were 29,533 organ transplants in 2014. That's a lot of transplants–your transplant won't be the first.

When you get to the hospital, depending on your health, there's a good chance you'll have to wait a little. You will be admitted and then wait in a hospital room for a certain amount of time (the waiting time can vary). Your nurse should be able to give you an estimated time frame of how long you will wait, so don't hesitate to ask.

You may not be excited to wait, but there are a couple of things they will need to do that will help the time pass. During this time they will get you suited in your hospital gown, start an IV and get it ready for your operation.

The wait, in addition to fasting for your operation, can cause your anxiety levels to rise. But try to relax during this time. Read, watch TV, pray, talk with your friends and family that are there, and ask all the questions you can think of. If there are any questions, concerns, or anything you want to know that might ease your mind make sure to ask. The last thing you need to be doing in this time is worrying about the details [Reminder: *RELAX*].

Instead of waiting anxiously in fear, think of this as a special time. In the face of a major operation it can be hard to look forward to the approaching moment with joy. But that is exactly how you should view this surgery. This transplant is going to allow you to become the healthy person you have hoped to become. Believe you are going to come through this stronger, healthier, and ready to take on the next chapter of your life.

Momentarily your nurse will come get you and inform you that the surgery team is ready. This time is all about you. So if you aren't comfortable, tell them. If you are cold, you should let the nurse know that you are cold. It will most likely take a few minutes for them to navigate you to the operating room. Depending on the procedures of the hospital, they may have to go over a couple more things before taking you into the operating room. As you enter the big, white room, you once again must remind yourself: relax. Take a deep breath and remember that this is a big step toward something great. This is not a step back, but rather a step forward into becoming the stronger, healthier version of you.

Your anesthesiologist will be one of the first people to greet you and begin speaking with you. This person is your friend. The anesthesiologist is the one who sends you off to sleep and makes sure you remain that way throughout your operation. Transplant surgeries are performed using a general anesthesia, so you will be completely unconscious throughout your operation.

Once you've been assisted onto the table, they will continue to ask you if you are comfortable. If ever you feel the slightest annoyance with the table or anything else, be sure to let them know. Once you are in place on the table, the anesthesiologist will place an oxygen mask on your face.

The oxygen flowing through the mask will help you relax before you are completely asleep.

After you are lying on the table your surgeon will come speak with you and talk you through the proceedings. After he has spoken with you the anesthesiologist will come back over and explain how you'll soon be falling asleep and how it will happen.

By now you should be feeling comfortable and nearly ready to fall asleep due to the oxygen you have been breathing through your mask. Soon, you will feel a warm sensation going through the site of your IV and into your body. This is perfectly normal. That warm sensation you feel is the general anesthesia moving through your IV and will soon cause you to fall asleep. However, before they allow you to fall asleep completely, the anesthesiologist will tell you to start counting down from 10. But believe me, with all the operations I have had, you probably won't make it to one. I challenge you to make it to 6.

Post-Transplant

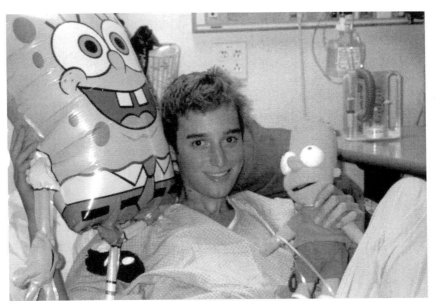

A couple of my visitors during my hospital stay in St. Louis.

CHAPTER 3:
Coming out of the Operation and Waking Up

"The hardships that I encountered in the past
will help me succeed in the future."

-Philip Emeagwali

Movies and television shows can be slightly misleading in the way they portray a major operation. Your transplant is not a long nap in which you will be dreaming. When you wake up, you won't feel the same as you do when waking up after several hours of sleep.

Although you may have been unconscious the past 6 to 8 hours, you won't feel rested as you come out of surgery. The past several hours of anesthesia-induced sleep is not a natural type of rest. "The reason you don't come out of transplant feeling rested is because of the general anesthesia used during the operation," explains Dr. Matt Yezerski of Nashville Office-Based Anesthesia. Dr. Yezerski goes on to describe, "being under" general anesthesia to be more like a coma than sleep. But don't let that alarm you. Your anesthesiologist keeps your body immobilized to keep you safe and to allow your surgeon to do his or her job.

As you begin to wake up you may feel a little confused, groggy, and slightly disoriented as the anesthesia begins to wear off. But don't let this worry you. This is all very normal and the cloudy state of mind will begin to fade. Your anesthesiologist has made sure that your body is ready to wake up. However, you may have the desire to go right back to sleep after waking up due to all the stress your body has gone through while you were sleeping. If the lights above your bed are too harsh make sure to ask that they be turned down. Your eyes might be a little sensitive for a few moments after waking up.

After your surgery, it is common to spend your first day or two in the intensive care unit. This is a normal practice; don't be alarmed when you wake up in the ICU. They keep you in the intensive care unit to keep a close eye on your progress before transferring you to a regular hospital room.

Upon waking from surgery, I remember it was only a brief moment before my nurse stopped into my room. It will take you a few minutes to collect your thoughts after you wake up from surgery. Your nurse will stop by simply to introduce him or herself and take your vital signs. Don't feel like you need to be carrying on a full conversation at this point. I don't even know if I was forming complete sentences within the first ten minutes. All I could think about was going back to bed. But as soon as that thought crossed my mind, my entire transplant team entered my room.

Questions

I felt guilty when my doctors asked if I had questions and had none to ask. With so much information being thrown at me, there were times I truly couldn't think of any questions. Often, I was just trying to wrap my mind around everything I was being told. But there were also times that I had a question sitting in the front of my mind, but I didn't want to ask for whatever reason.

I would encourage you to ask any question that comes to mind. No matter how minor it may seem, don't hesitate to ask your questions. I know that our teachers, parents, and every other person of authority have said, at one time or another, "there is no such thing as a dumb question." But it is very true, and even more accurate when it pertains to your health. There were times that I would keep my questions to myself because I assumed I should have known the answer. Something similar might happen to you. Maybe a question will come to mind that's previously been discussed but you're unable to recall. If that is the case and your doctor has told you four times before, go ahead and ask the same question for the fifth time. If it is a concern you have in regards to your health, you should know the answer (it might be a good idea to write it down after the fifth time).

There may come a time that a question pops into your head and you just don't feel comfortable asking your doctor, nurse, or coordinator. An easy fix is to find someone that would feel comfortable asking the question for you. This might be a parent who asks the doctor on your behalf or maybe a different member of your transplant team with whom you are more comfortable with.

Your diet

As your body begins to wake up so will your appetite. For liver transplant patients, this indicates that your liver is working. Dr. Shepherd explains the reason for this intense hunger during your first week out of surgery: "Most patients start off undernourished and starved for a few days after the transplant: the new liver has to "wake up." One of the liver's important functions is to act as energy storage for the body. The transplanted liver is depleted of energy, and has to recover from the removal and preservation injury. It takes about 6 weeks for this to occur usually, and during this time it is busy regenerating, and getting up to speed from an energy point of view."

During your stay in the intensive care unit, you will not be eating solid foods. Some of it depends on your individual experience, but, as already stated, the only thing I started out ingesting was the moisture from sponges. After a while I was able to have ice chips. But do not expect a four-course meal during your stay in the ICU. Not to scare you (rather to prepare you), but it was three days after my transplant before I could eat anything. My first meal was a glorious experience after those 72 hours. It wasn't the cheeseburger and fries I had been dreaming of, but after three days of sponges and ice chips, the meal of Jell-O and chicken broth was close enough.

According to Mayo Clinic, you most likely will remain in the ICU for 48 to 72 hours. However, your doctor will be able to give you an estimated time of how long they expect you will stay in the ICU. Throughout this time your doctors and nurses will be closely monitoring you to see if you are showing any signs of rejection or complication.

Once your condition has stabilized, you will be moved into a room where you will most likely stay the remainder of your time in the hospital. Usually around this time is when you will be able to begin eating more solid foods. For several days an intravenous protein supplemented my caloric intake until I was consuming enough food on my own throughout the day. My doctors called it the "golden milkshake." Apparently, these were not Dairy Queen Blizzards running through my IV. My appetite did not come back automatically. There were times I had to force myself to eat. And when you have to force yourself to eat each meal every day for several days in a row, it gets old fast. But your appetite will come back. Until it does, you need to be intentional about eating each meal and making sure each day to consume the amount of calories specified by your transplant team. Your appetite may come and go, but it's important that you eat in order to maintain your body's strength. Even though you may not feel hungry your body still needs food to be able to heal.

My favorite girls in the entire world: my beautiful wife, Kara, and our pretty little girl, London.

CHAPTER 4:
The Importance of a Community and Letting Yourself Heal

"The key is to keep company only with people who uplift you, whose presence calls forth your best."

-*Epictetus*

No one denies the significant impact relationships have on a person's life. They are an essential part of day-to-day living. In all stages of life, human interaction is an undeniable necessity that should not be overlooked. At times our relationships can be our greatest source of frustration, but more often they are one of our greatest suppliers of strength. Your friends and family are the ones you celebrate with in the joyful experiences, and likewise they are the ones you grieve with during the trials of life. I believe that in order to excel through life, you must have family and friends to share it with.

Now, more than ever, these relationships will play a vital role. I know they will prove to be an undeniable benefit throughout your transplant. Mentally, relationships provide support when the experience becomes too heavy to endure. Physically, they offer a shoulder to cry on or an ear to listen when you need to get something off your chest. Emotionally, they supply strength when you reach your wit's end. We draw strength from relationships and are fueled by the energy they impart.

As you continue through this experience, it is important that you keep your loved ones close so they can speak into your life and to provide you strength in your journey. There will be times of great success and they will be there to celebrate with you. Likewise there will be times of discouragement and they will be there to embrace those moments with you as well. I don't know if I can fully express how important the words of encouragement, notes, and get-well cards were to my recovery process. Each one acted as a vitamin of strength to carry me forward.

The relationships within my support group consisted of a few different levels of closeness depending on how well I knew each person. The nature of my interaction within each relationship depends upon how close I am to the individual, so it will be as you look to these individuals for support on your road to recovery. Your immediate family and maybe a couple close friends will be the ones you rely on for all of your struggles. These are the ones you have laughed with, cried with, and shared your most personal details with.

I was fortunate to have my family each step of the way throughout my transplant experience. They were a daily source of encouragement, and I hope your family will be there to support you as well. However, you must realize that they are going through an extremely hard time as well. I am certain there were times my mother experienced more pain than I felt. You should acknowledge what your family is also going through in this time. Sympathetically, they will go through a great deal of emotional and mental stress as you go through your transplant. There are times that this can even manifest itself in the form of physical pain. The patient is obviously the one experiencing it first-hand, but the family suffers alongside the patient as well. Support those who are supporting you.

I come from a big family and so I was blessed to have a large built-in support group around me. Not all of them were able to be at the hospital when I woke up, but it was comforting to wake up, after the operation, to the familiar faces that could come. With several hundred miles in between my hospital and home, daily family visits were not feasible. Nonetheless, they came to visit every chance they had. My mom, however, stayed with me throughout my entire stay in the hospital and the weeks to follow when I remained in close proximity to the hospital.

Someone to share with

I would encourage you to find someone with whom you can share your heart. Someone who can be the emotional support that you will often need throughout your transplant. Most likely you already have someone in mind, but if you don't, then I encourage you to choose someone. You might choose one of your friends or a family member to be that person. It may be someone you have to call on the phone, but it is a healthy practice to be able to share your heart and mind with someone.

This is a relationship that you need to feel safe in: a relationship that allows you to let your guard down. The reason I say that is because in times of great hurt, whether physical or emotional, you need to be able to express your true emotions. For me, this person was my mom. Often, she couldn't relate to what I was going through or what I was thinking. But she was with me each step of the way and saw the highs, as well as the lows. First-hand she experienced my victories such as the first steps I took around my hospital room, then the hospital floor, and then around the entire hospital as my strength progressed. However, she also had a front row seat during the hardest moments.

As I explained earlier, you have different types of relationships. Each one is based on a level of interaction: how tightly woven the relationship is and how much support you receive from it. Your immediate family and close friends will be the ones you rely on for the majority of your strength and encouragement throughout your journey. These are the relationships that will sustain you, provide needed encouragement, and keep you focused. These relationships represent the people you hold most dear: the select few allowed into the deepest areas of your life. Continue to allow these people full access. I found that it was a natural tendency to shut people out of particular moments of my transplant journey. But that was often when I needed their support the most. Continue to share your heart with those you are closest to. It is good to have someone who is with you each step of the way, who cares about each hurt and every victory you go through.

In addition to those whom you are closest, you will have the rest of your family and other friends who you are not as close with. These are the people who will provide a more surface level encouragement, who will send you a card, or stop by with an uplifting word to brighten your day. I call it surface level encouragement only because they don't know the full extent of what you are going through. They know of what you are going through as an outsider looking in, but they do not fully understand what you are experiencing like those closest to you. The get-well cards and encouraging visits I received from such individuals was a welcomed relief each day. These conversations caused me to remain focused on my recovery. They helped me envision what life would be like once I got out of the hospital.

There will also be the people you do not know very well, such as friends of the family or distant relatives—people you may have only heard of or seen once or twice before. Their visits may not always be timely or even convenient, and at times, you may see their presence only as a distraction from your afternoon nap schedule. But I discovered that when I allowed myself to look past that, I often found these visits to be very encouraging. They helped break up the monotony of my daily routine. It's always a blessing to know that you are in the minds of others, and when someone will go out of their way to pay you a visit, it makes you feel special. And everyone wants to feel special.

I can remember waking up from a nap one afternoon, to my mom talking with a young couple that I didn't recognize. They didn't look familiar and from what I gathered from the conversation, I'd never met them. As soon as my eyes were fully open, I remember the gentleman greeting me with a warm smile, but he never gave me his name. He then quickly handed me a gift that he had brought. I still had no idea who he was and I wasn't about to ask my mom in front of them, "Mom, who are these random people in my hospital room?" He asked how I was feeling, followed by a few words of encouragement. Throughout the conversation I was still waking up, so I was never able to pinpoint how I knew the couple. The sincerity with which he spoke made me think I should know him.

No matter how hard I tried, I couldn't recall meeting the couple. But before the two left, the gentleman handed me a signed football and told me to get well soon. It was Brandon Manumaleuna, the tight end for the St. Louis Rams. Unfortunately, without his name or number splashed across his back, I was unable to recognize who he was. I had never been a big St. Louis Rams fan, but since that day they've held a special place in my heart. Beyond that, I could tell you several stories of unexpected visitors who were rays of sunshine in otherwise cloudy days. Each one taking time out of their day to provide a much needed boost of encouragement to mine.

In addition to the support group you surround yourself with, allow yourself to develop relationships with your coordinators, doctors, and nurses. Each of them will be with you every step of the way for the next several weeks, and your coordinator and doctors even beyond that. Many of these people I kept up with for years after my transplant and still do to this day. They will become some of your biggest supporters. A victory for you means a victory for them.

Is this going to be the same type of connection you share with your family or close friends? No. Nor am I saying that you have to become pen pals after your transplant. But I would encourage a friendly relationship all the same. It is far more enjoyable to be the patient that is liked by your doctor than disliked. Beyond making your life and theirs' more pleasant, there are many reasons that it is in your best interest to befriend each of these individuals. One of the reasons is that you are far more likely to trust a friend when they tell you to do something (especially the things you aren't so excited about) or give you advice.

I can remember, on several different occasions, one of my doctors coming into my room and telling me I had to be eating more during the time when eating was neither easy nor enjoyable. But when that direction came from a doctor I had been able to get to know, it was an order I was more willing to accept. Obviously you won't get to know all of your doctors like this, but I would certainly recommend taking the time to get to know your transplant coordinator. Your coordinator is someone you will get to know better than the rest of your transplant team, whether you like it or not.

The doctors and nurses, who may be the hardest on you, can also be a wealth of encouragement. I could never sleep on the pillows that were provided by the hospital. No matter how hard I tried, the plastic lining always made my head too warm. The pillow seemed to act like one of those sweat suits you see people wearing in the sauna. Thankfully, one of the nurses on my floor heard how particular I was about my pillow. With this in mind, he supplied me with softer, more comfortable pillows. My new pillows were like an oasis for my head compared to the plastic-encased cotton swabs I had been sleeping on before.

To this day, I have never forgotten that. A new pillow may seem like a trivial detail, but it made a huge difference in how I was able to sleep. And sleep is an essential key to recovery. Beyond a caregiver, this nurse became a daily source of encouragement.

Although they may be the ones to push you and even sometimes annoy you, I want to remind you that your transplant team is on your side through this journey. Listen to them, heed their advice, and take the time to get to know them.

Allow your body to heal: don't rush

There is a certain step-by-step recovery process your body must go through during your time of healing. This process may not look the same for everyone and the time line may be different for each person, but there is a recovery ladder your body must climb in sequential order without missing the rungs in between. Trying to force your body to skip to the next rung before completing the prior can be detrimental to your healing process.

There are occasions and times when you can push yourself but there are times you need to patiently allow your body to work. You must listen to your body in each circumstance in order to know what it is telling you. Healing is a delicate process and during this time of recovery you need to learn to relax, allow your body to run a certain course of healing, and listen to the direction provided by your doctors. As stated by my former liver transplant coordinator, Lyn Bianchi, "Take it one hour at a time. There are going to be ups and downs. Your first year is like a roller coaster: you are doing well then hit a bump, slide back, and have to get back up the hill. But your transplant team is there to help with these situations and it is *normal* to have these bumps."

There are things that you will be faced with that are very common and shouldn't cause you to worry although they may catch you off guard. I was faced with more than a few setbacks during my recovery process, but this was one of the reasons a more open relationship with my coordinator and doctors was beneficial. I trusted they had my best interest in mind. My successful transplant and recovery was a victory for them as well.

Prior to surgery when my doctors spoke of rejection I had determined that I was not going to allow this to happen. My doctors assured me that it was common to face a period of rejection shortly after transplant. They assured me they would be ready if it happened. But I was still determined that I wasn't going to experience any rejection. In spite of my determination, shortly after my transplant my doctor came in with my most recent blood work results and, sure enough, I was facing my first phase of rejection. But, reminding me of a pre-operation discussion, my doctor reassured me that this was common. With the proper medication schedule implemented, they would get it under control.

In these times it is natural to be frustrated. At times you may feel like you've taken a couple steps backwards and the light at the end of the tunnel is fading instead of getting brighter. But don't become discouraged. Although the early days of recovery may seem slower with minimal progress, the days will soon come when your strength will return: getting up to take a few steps across your room will progress into taking strides around the hospital floor. And soon after that you may find yourself taking long hikes around the entire hospital.

Do not let the day-to-day frustrations get the best of you. Lean on your support group during these times, and realize that each of these steps, even the ones that seem to take you backwards, are an integral part of your journey to recovery. I recall the moments when I would wonder to myself if I would ever have the energy or strength to walk more than a few feet at a time. As soon as a thought like that crossed my mind I made sure to take it captive. Don't allow those thoughts to sink any deeper than that. This type of thinking is not worth the energy you use to entertain it. Your body is getting stronger, even when you don't think it is, and it's continuing to recover… even when you don't think it is. Smother each of those negative thoughts with positive determination in place of it. Remind yourself that you are going to leave this hospital. Sooner than you think, you are going to be back to yourself, but a stronger, healthier version of yourself this time.

In regards to the support groups previously referenced, the positive reinforcement they speak into your life will help prevent such negative thoughts from getting the best of you. Another good way to turn such thoughts on their head is to surround yourself with inspiration. From the people who are around you to the books you read, the music you listen to, and even the movies that you watch–submerse yourself in positive reinforcement.

Another exercise worth practicing is setting goals. However, your goals must be realistic and should not get in the way of a healthy recovery. In a few chapters, I will talk more about goal setting and the importance of having goals to focus on, but depending upon your personality and your level of drive, your goals can get in the way of a safe, healthy recovery. A healthy goal to set immediately after transplant would be to walk around your hospital floor. An unrealistic goal would be to immediately try walking around the entire hospital. As you are on this journey, you need to be cautious to take the appropriate steps in acquiring your health. It won't come over night, but it will come. You must set goals within reason and without rushing yourself. This is especially important in the early days. Before setting your sights on running a marathon, first focus on things such as taking short walks, your breathing, eating, and daily fluid intake.

Don't needlessly rush your body's healing process. Be determined and remain focused on recovery. Walter Elliot, the Scottish politician, once wisely noted, "Perseverance is not a long race; it is many short races one after the other." So do not be discouraged if one of your races is longer than another. Focus on the goal you are currently working towards and persevere through it into the next.

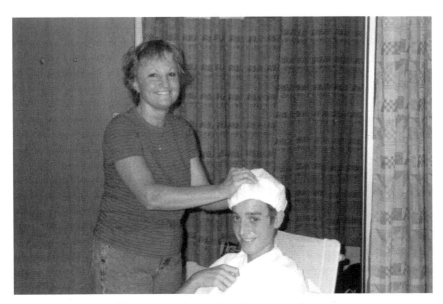

I may not have been able to take a shower for a few weeks after transplant, but these shower caps, pre-packed with soap, were a pretty good substitute.

CHAPTER 5:
Medications and Things to Comfort

"Life is 10% what happens to me and
90% of how I react to it."

-John Maxwell

The importance of medications: they serve a purpose... trust me

I've been told that the two most difficult things to communicate to a transplant patient are the importance of taking medications and getting blood work done. There is no way around it; your medications are a necessity. Taking your medications should not be considered a suggestion or something you'll get around to when it's most convenient. Your medications are essential to your health and it's mandatory you take them at the times your doctor specifies. They may seem like a burden at first. This is especially true when you feel like you have an entire pharmacy worth of pills to swallow each morning after breakfast. But your doctor has explained the importance of why you must take your medications and it is imperative that you take it to heart.

Transplant patients typically start out taking several different medications. The medications will vary depending on what type of transplant you had. Some of the medications are new after surgery and some may be continued from before. You might take certain medications multiple times a day and some on a different schedule. Your transplant team may have to change medications or adjust dosages several times in order to find the combination that works best for you.

The thought might not cross your mind while you are still in the hospital, but at one point or another you will probably entertain the thought, even if it is just for a moment, of what would happen if you were to stop taking your medications. If we were honest, all of us transplant patients would admit to processing this thought at some point. As long as that's where it stops, there's no harm. It doesn't hurt to think it through as long as it causes you to realize the importance of your medications. Those who have been harmed are the transplant patients who get three months, six months, one year, or more out of transplant and see their medications as a nuisance. They stop taking them because they don't truly realize how vitally important their medications are to their well-being. You must place a high priority on taking each dose of medication at the specified time. After your transplant, your medications are fundamentally important to your health.

All the medications that you currently take serve an essential purpose to your health. Your anti-rejection medications are, most likely, the drugs you will be taking for the longest amount of time. I want to drive home their importance so that you do not miss the point and make the grave mistake too many have made in the past.

To illustrate the purpose of your anti-rejection medications, you could say your body continually needs convincing to allow this new resident to live within it. The human body is an incredible thing. It was created with a very unique self-defense mechanism known as your immune system. It is essential for life. When something enters your body that is not supposed to be there or was not there originally, your body is going to try to get rid of it as soon as possible. Similar to the way stadium security guards won't grant access to people without tickets. However, your body's security system goes one step further. It acts as both the security system and the self-defense instrument. After your brain has been alerted that there is an "intruder" within the body, the brain sends out signals to eradicate this intruder. Your body is a very hostile environment toward the intruder and will immediately work to kill that which is uninvited. Think of the last time you had a splinter in your finger. If you were unable to pull it out with a tweezers, your body eventually pushed it out on its own.

The way the body's immune system works is an amazing process. Unfortunately, the way it is wired makes it an unreceptive environment to your new organ. Thankfully with the advances of modern medicine, your anti-rejection medications allow your new organ to live within your body.

Shortly after my liver transplant, while still in the hospital, I experienced the importance of ant-rejection medications first-hand. It was an unfortunate education, but a vivid reminder that has stuck with me all these years since it occurred. I share this story with you not to frighten you, but rather prevent you from making the same mistake.

During my recovery in the hospital, there was a young man in the room next to me who was battling a severe case of rejection. He decided, on his own, that he no longer needed to take his medications. His reasoning, however, seemed quite logical. He was a liver transplant recipient who had recovered and was back to a normal life. As I mentioned earlier, once you reach a certain point after your transplant, a tempting thought arises. After you're feeling well, you may feel like you no longer have a need for taking medications. Taking the medications made sense when you were in the hospital and didn't feel well, but now that you feel better you start to think, "Why would a person who feels good need to be taking medication?" That is the temptation.

Dr. Lowell points out two of the common reasons patients neglect their medications after surgery. The first reason patients stop taking their medications is because they are feeling better. Once their strength and energy returns they no longer see the need to be taking medications. But a patient must realize that in order to continue to heal and feel better he or she must continue taking the medications prescribed by the doctor.

The second reason many patients stop taking their medications is that they see the act of taking medication a nuisance. They simply view their medications as an inconvenience when they have re-entered normal life. This is especially true in teens and young adults. It's easy to take medications in the hospital and at home. But it's when you are out in public, with friends, or on a date that it becomes an annoyance. In these settings, we often fear being viewed differently and so we make every provision to be like those around us. However, before this even becomes an issue, you must commit to taking your medications even when it's inconvenient. Always keep a dose in your pocket and allow yourself to slip away (even if it's a quick trip to the restroom… everyone has to go to the bathroom at some point in the night) for a moment to take the medication.

Sadly, my fellow liver transplant patient did not heed these warnings. By the time his doctors discovered what was happening, his rejection had become too severe, and were unable to reverse the effects of the prolonged rejection. My third day on the hospital floor was his last. It is a heartbreaking story, but I hope it instills a healthy apprehension in order to keep you from neglecting such a simple, yet important daily task. Don't let the inconvenience of taking medications cloud the vital purpose they serve.

If you have not already, I can almost guarantee you will run into someone who will tell you of a friend of a friend or someone else they know who was able to get off of his or her medications. Or maybe you will even run into a person who personally was able to get off of all their medications.

I don't want to discourage you, remove the hope of, or make you think you won't be able to get off your medications. There are patients who are able to get off their medications. However, simply stated: do not let that become your main objective. Your body's recovery and continued health should remain your top priority.

They say it requires thirty days to turn a practice into a habit. But I am not going to attempt to sugar coat it. Taking your medications can be annoying at first. I can remember back in high school that I was almost always running out the door in the afternoon only to run back in to grab my medications for later that night so I would have them with me. But I promise, in time, that it becomes much easier remembering to take your medications throughout the day.

Soon it will become second nature. A practice that proved helpful for me was placing a backup set of morning and evening pills in my car and even in my coat pocket. It will prevent you from having to scramble to get back home if you're caught without your meds or worse, going without them for the night. You can find little pill sized plastic bags in most drug stores so you won't have to carry around a large sandwich sized plastic bag or the entire pill bottle in your pocket. Do everything you can to make it a natural part of your life. It should flow within your daily schedule.

At this point in my life, taking my medications at 8:00 am and then again twelve hours later at 8:00 pm has become routine. However, if you are frustrated, at times, by the large number of pills you are forced to take, be encouraged that this number will start to decrease. I am down to only having to take two medications at this point, and each one is a very minimal dose.

Taking medications is part of your life now. Find a way to make it a seamless element of your daily routine so that it becomes natural and not an inconvenience.

Things of comfort: make yourself as comfortable as possible

In addition to developing a support group, not being in a rush, and taking your medications, I recommend doing everything you can to make your hospital stay as comfortable as possible. Your hospital room is a good place to start. I know what you're probably thinking, and I agree that hospital rooms are not the most comfortable places in the world, but there are things you can do to improve the atmosphere in your hospital room. When you are more comfortable you are able to relax, and when you are able to relax your body is able to heal.

Your hospital room

There are many different ways to make your room a more soothing place to live in while you're in the hospital. I developed a few different habits during my stay in the hospital. Some of them may sound strange to an outside observer, but the important thing about each of these habits was that they made me more comfortable and allowed me to relax a little more.

One of the habits that stuck with me for several years after my transplant was sleeping with six to eight pillows in my bed. It started with the two pillows I brought from home. I've always traveled with my own pillow. Right along with my toothbrush, I don't go on a trip without it. And going to the hospital wasn't any different.

My pillows provided a sense of comfort. They had the smell of home and they reminded me of sleeping in my own bed. I had also lost fifty pounds that I couldn't spare to begin with. I needed as much extra padding as I could find. The multiple pillows created a nest-like environment that cradled my body.

In addition to my strange obsession with pillows, I had cravings like a pregnant woman during my recovery. As odd as it may be, I didn't just crave the taste of food like most people crave, I also wanted to smell certain scents. One in particular was the scent of powder laundry detergent.

I will admit, it sounds incredibly strange. With such a strange habit you may wonder whether I was in the hospital for a transplant or psychiatric treatment. But you may take comfort in knowing that there is perfect explanation for the strange cravings and habits you acquire in the hospital. My pillows represented a sense of security and while going through a transplant; security is a very important thing. The strange appetite and cravings come from the things your new organ is depleted of. Dr. Shepherd describes this as a sign of being undernourished as you come out of transplant. If you are craving a certain food, there is a good chance it represents something your body is lacking. Although I'm still not sure what my body was lacking that caused me to enjoy smelling powder laundry detergent.

But if it is not harming you, and the habit creates a certain amount of comfort, than why not? My obsession for the smell of laundry detergent only lasted about a week. I no longer keep a container of Tide next to my bed.

Beyond my pillows and my container of Tide, I used many other methods to keep me comfortable. I'm a big fan of movies, so naturally, friends and family were constantly bringing me movies to watch. One of the best gifts I received in the hospital was the first three seasons of the Simpsons from my aunt and uncle. I received enough books to start my own, public library during my stay in the hospital, and I never got tired of receiving books. However, the not-so-educational gifts were the best.

The things that provide you peace and solitude can come in almost any form. Only you truly know what is going to make you most comfortable and help put you at ease. I spoke with someone who said his comfort during his hospital stay was the lamp he had in his hospital room. He never used the normal lights in the room (except when needed by the hospital staff), but chose to use the light from the couple different lamps he had brought with him because they reminded him of home. It was a more comfortable alternative to the lights already in the room.

For years, research has proven the powerful benefits music can have on a person's physical, mental, and emotional states. Depending on the genre and the way you react, music can help you relax and even be a source of encouragement. As long as it's okay with everyone, you may choose to play it throughout your room or through a pair of headphones.

Another way to infuse joy into your hospital room is by placing photographs around your bed. With the advancement of modern technologies such as smart phones and tablets, your photographs are never more than a couple clicks away. However, I encourage you to go one step further and print out a few of those photos and place them around your room.

Photographs are a great way to lift your spirit and brighten your day. You may choose to display photographs of friends you look forward to spending time with or places you look forward to visiting.

You may even choose to lay out a picture or two of a place you have always dreamed of visiting. Maybe there is a tropical island you've wanted to see, possibly a historic landmark you've wanted to visit, or even a mountain you've wanted to climb. Or maybe your pictures represent goals you're determined to reach.

Next to the pictures of my family, I had in my hospital room, were cutout images of basketball shoes. Pages torn from sports magazines and athletic catalogues, they represented my goal of becoming healthy again. I dreamed of the day I would be able to play a game of pickup basketball again.

In addition to what you hear, see, and feel in your room, don't over-look the sense of smell. I already mentioned how important smell was to my stay in the hospital. I'm not advising you to light candles in your hospital room, but you may enjoy the aroma of an unlit candle, clothing from home, or freshly baked cookies to fill the air in your room.

During my recovery, I cherished anything that smelled like home. I remember how sad I was when my pillowcases had to be washed. Before that, each time I buried my head in my pillow I was immediately taken back to my bedroom at home. A t-shirt that smells like home or a pillowcase that reminds you of your own house may seems trivial, but sometimes it is the smallest thing that makes all the difference.

This photo was taken at my two-year check-up with my
transplant doctor, Dr. Ross Shepherd.

CHAPTER 6:
Looking to the Future

"Dream as if you'll live forever. Live as if you'll die today."

-James Dean

After transplant

I have heard many people refer to life after transplant as the "new normal." They're referring to some of the possible adjustments after transplant. Things like taking your anti-rejection medications, being careful with your suppressed immune system, and any other differences you may encounter.

I remember the first time I heard post-transplant life described in this way, and to be completely honest, it scared me. It gave me the idea that I would have to live a limited version of the life I was living prior to becoming sick. As if I had to change my expectations of life.

It is absolutely a new normal compared to the way you have been feeling leading up to the transplant. Most likely you have been worn out, tired, and frustrated. But after transplant those symptoms will begin to dissolve. You will not feel like a million bucks the moment you step out of transplant. It will take some time for your body to heal and recover. But as your health begins to improve you will begin to feel more energized, and stronger.

The recovery process doesn't look the same for each patient. It's not a black and white, cookie-cutter process that can be specifically mapped out for everyone. The soreness you may experience after surgery may last for several months. As a liver transplant patient, I remember how sore my ribs were after the transplant and they remained sore for several months. But the soreness won't last, it will become less and less until it dissolves completely. Everyone's body responds in its own unique way.

It will depend upon the operation you have, but realize your first year could have several ups and downs. If you go into the process knowing this, you'll likely be much less frustrated if your recovery doesn't happen overnight. In my recovery I feel as though I crossed two different milestones: one at six months, and the second after one year.

After the first six months I felt like the majority of my energy had returned and I was able to do most of the activities I wanted to a certain extent. I will let you in on a little secret of mine. I have been a big advocate of the gym for many years, however, after I got home from my transplant I knew I was not ready for the gym. I wanted to be able to workout, but I knew I was not prepared for the intensity or pressure that would be present in a gym setting. In order to get back in shape, I bought two dumbbells and a simple workout video. It allowed me to re-develop some of the strength I had lost over the past several months in the comfort of my own home. I did this just until I developed enough strength and energy to feel comfortable enough to go back to the gym.

After one year I felt as though a large amount of my strength that I had before becoming sick had returned. I don't think this happened automatically though. I worked hard to restore my strength throughout that first year. I made sure to follow the guidelines that my doctor had established and that included taking my medications even when I didn't want to, getting my lab work and other tests completed, working out, and following any other guidelines my doctor had established. If you come out of your transplant determined that you are going to make a great recovery then I believe you will. A lot of your recovery will come down to placing mind over matter.

On your road to recovery, don't get ahead of yourself. Listen to your body. Be determined to remain on this road, but as you are pushing yourself forward be quick to read the signs your body reveals. Depending on how aggressive you are, over-extending yourself can become a problem. Don't push yourself too hard.

My leash

Throughout the beginning of my recovery there were times I felt like I was on a leash. Fearing that if I walked too close to the line my doctor had drawn, I would get sick again. Like a fragile vase, I felt like I had to be careful with myself so that I wouldn't "break." I was overwhelmed by everything I had to remember for my own healthcare after I got out of the hospital. I had a suppressed immune system so I had to be careful around crowds. I was on several different medications and so I had to remember which one to take at the specific times I was supposed to take it. At times, I felt like I had a collar around my neck and was connected to a leash that was preventing me from living my life to the fullest. But with time as I learned to take care of myself I settled in to my life and the chokehold feeling began to fade away.

With time, it all becomes very natural. Following the direction of your doctors will lead to life becoming easier and more comfortable. Your medications will become fewer, the dosage will become less, and you won't always have to wear a mask when you go outside. I would be rich if I was given a nickel for every time someone said, "Wow! I never would have guessed you had a liver transplant." It's a compliment because it reminds me of how far I've come.

As my former physician, Dr. Lowell once informed me—it comes down to common sense and good judgment. He offers these six points of advice for patients coming out of transplant:

1. Stay as strong as possible
    Maintain muscle strength and fitness.

2. Nutrition

    Eat a healthy diet (advice that anyone who wants to be healthy should listen to).

3. Build strong social support/network

    Keep your family and friends close—there is strength in numbers.

4. Decide who your point of contact will be for your transplant team

    If your point of contact is your transplant coordinator, be sure to stay in contact with him or her.

5. Take your pills even after you feel healthy

    ALWAYS take your pills. This means even after you have fully recovered and feel healthy. Never stop taking your pills. This also means that you still need to take your pills when it feels awkward because no one else takes pills or you are on a date. When I was still becoming comfortable with taking my medications in public, I would often sneak away to the bathroom and take them before returning. If you are not comfortable taking your medication in front of others, then slip away and take them in privacy. There is nothing wrong with that. But do not allow that to become an excuse for neglecting to take your medications. They are vital to your health.

6. Become an advocate

    Most likely you have had someone speak into your life (speaking words of encouragement) at one point or another throughout your transplant experience. Do the same for someone else. Share your story.

I'm now in the best shape of my life and I've never felt better. You need to find a healthy balance that works for you. This is your life now and you have the responsibility to live it out and live it to the fullest. Don't take unnecessary risks, but also don't become an apprehensive germaphobe. Take the necessary precautions that are within your control. Wash your hands before you eat and after touching unclean surfaces. Yes, you may find it beneficial to have a bottle of hand sanitizer with you at all times.

One of the biggest precautions I took came to flying on airplanes. I started preparing myself for each flight I took, and I still do to this day in preparation. I always make sure to have eaten a solid, healthy meal before the flight along with consuming a large amount of water. I continue drinking fluids throughout the flight. I've discovered that the meal I eat before the flight gives my body the strength it needs to fight off anything I might be coming in contact with throughout the flight. And the fluids help flush out anything I've interacted with that could potentially make me sick. Finding ways to assist your suppressed immune system is always a great idea. But realize that everyone gets sick every once in a while. Even people who haven't had a transplant get sick throughout the year. So when you do catch a cold or feel sick, don't be hard on yourself. Use common sense and good judgment and take the necessary precautions that are within your control.

Discouragement vs. perseverance and the obstacles we encounter

Pre-transplant, post-transplant, and any other time in life will yield some form of discouragement. Whether it's the limitations you sense, the sickness you battle, the recovery process you experience, or any other obstacle you encounter, life is never without barriers. But it's what you do with them that will determine your fate. In my experience, discouragement seems to work like a fire. The more I fuel it the more it consumes me. But when I starve it I begin to see the flame shrink.

Discouragement is toxic to your recovery process and will choke the potential from your ability to persevere. One of the greatest fuels you can throw on the fire of discouragement is allowing self-pity to creep in. When you begin feeling sorry for yourself it will cloud your view of everything happening around you. It will cause you to see your victories as insignificant events and your failures to seem cataclysmic. Everyone has thrown their own one-man pity party at some point in life, but nothing good has ever come from a celebration of sorrow.

It is in that moment that you must choose to be strong. Do not allow the pity to persist. If you see your self-sympathy streamers being hung or smell your personal compassion-cake being baked, put an end to it immediately!

A phrase I have often heard tossed around in the athletic arena is "dig deep." It is a matter of finding the will and perseverance to do so. You have the will inside of you, but you need to dig deep enough until you find it. You now must make a habit out of perseverance. If you will begin to persevere, it will compound itself. Perseverance breeds perseverance. I've noticed in my own life when I'm committed to eating healthy (thanks to the encouragement from my beautiful wife), it becomes much easier for me to continue eating healthy after I've started. But it begins with the choice to be committed to the cause.

Commit yourself to perseverance and don't allow discouragement to take hold of you. Take a deep breath, shrug the discouragement from your shoulders, and press on towards your goal one little step at a time. Persevere… emotionally, physically, and mentally. When discouragement is telling you to quit, feel bad for yourself, and give up, keep digging deeper until that voice is drowned out. If you dig deep enough and long enough you will hear a voice saying "you can."

Obstacles

In this journey, consider yourself a soldier fighting your way to victory. When it comes to those who've been tested by battle, you will rarely find one on the other side of the struggle without the marks to prove what he has gone through. But each mark that the battle leaves imprinted is a tally to the measure of your strength that you now possess. Let your scars be the evidence of your strength of character.

Several months after my liver transplant, when I was out of the proverbial woods, I stopped and looked back at the path that lay behind me. I envisioned myself having just stepped out of a densely wooded forest. The forest was a picture of the trials I had just walked through. Now that I was in the clear, the branches of the trees no longer blocked out the light. The sun now poured down on my face; I was able to breathe a sigh of relief and carry on with life. I was encouraged, hopeful, and determined to take on the new path that lay before me.

In the culmination of all my experiences, I have found that life is made up of many stages. As you journey into recovery, you will find a chapter in your life coming to a close. It is a chapter that has played a large role in shaping you into the person you are now. Each chapter consists of different paths, joys, and battles that will be fought. Once you reach the end of one stage, another begins and life never allows you to stop. It continues to move forward without a plateau in time. As our 35th president, John F. Kennedy once said, "For time and the world do not stand still. Change is the law of life. And those who look only to the past or present are certain to miss the future."

On this journey you overcame obstacles, fought battles, and in spite of how you may feel physically, you are victorious. Because of the obstacles you have had to overcome you are now stronger than you were when you began this journey, with an unyielding determination live out each moment of each day. You know the value of your life, so *live and make the most of it!* I implore you to live more courageously and to dream more fearlessly!

Marks and mementos

You've gone through battle: a war waged against your health. Now that you stand on the other side, you wear the marks of battle. What am I referring to? Scars.

I hesitate to bring up the topic because people view their scars differently, but I know some who are very self-conscience about them. I know this because I was once self-conscience about mine. At first, I hesitated taking my shirt off at the pool. But then I remember a conversation I had. Someone once asked me if I was going to have plastic surgery. The question floated through my mind for a moment. I had never thought about plastic surgery.

After a moment of contemplation the idea settled in my mind. I was almost offended. Covering up or removing the evidence of my experience, I thought, would be cheating myself. My scar is a reminder of what I have gone through. I went through it and I was victorious. It's the physical evidence of the strength I have acquired along the way. But I realize that this type of thinking may not come naturally for some. And if that is the case, than I believe you should address the issue. I want to offer a few simple suggestions that might help you.

1. Address the issue: acknowledge that it bothers you and don't ignore it.
2. Talk to someone about it: don't allow your thoughts to get the best of you.
3. Be thankful for your health: it is a gift.
4. Stop thinking people are looking at you: if anything, the scar you wear makes you more unique and shows that you have an incredible story to share.
5. Be healthy: the healthier you are the better view you will have of yourself.
6. In time, learn to accept it.

Each mark that the battle leaves imprinted upon you is a tally to the measure of your strength that you now possess. Let your scars be the evidence of your strength and the determination of your will.

Dream

With regards to the significance of each of the topics discussed in this book, I believe this to be one of the most important. Since my liver transplant, I've had the opportunity to speak to different people who are either about to go down the road I traveled or are currently on it. I have spoken with the parents of patients, and I've also spoken with the patients themselves. I often see a certain type of concern in their eyes. A fear that their life will never be the same. They fear the "new normal" the doctor refers to, concerned it will cripple their dreams.

I think all patients who have gone through a major operation like this have felt that way at one time or another. The doctors always tell you how much better you will feel afterward and how much more energy you will have, but in the back of your mind you have your doubts.

"Will life really be the same as it was before I started feeling sick?"

"Will I really have all this energy that they tell me about?"

If you find yourself in one of the positions I previously mentioned, either looking down this road, or currently going down it, I want to answer those questions for you. "Yes!" The answer is yes. You can feel great. You can be healthy. You can become strong. Everyone's experience is different. As you have already heard, do not compare your transplant experience to anyone else's. But you don't have to be relegated to living a limited version of the life you dream of.

Just how much more energy will you have and how much better will you feel? Some of that is still to be determined, but I believe much of it is within your control. But it will not happen overnight. It may be a gradual increase over time. At the time of my transplant, my coordinator shared an interesting observation. Post-transplant patients often perform better in school because of their increased energy levels and their improved capacity to focus.

I'm not going to claim I turned into a straight-A student following my transplant. But naps became a thing of the past, my energy levels soon increased, and because of this I was able to focus better. A lot of this goes back to taking care of yourself. After transplant, you need to be even more determined to take care of your body. That means eating right, exercising, and taking the medications your doctor prescribes.

This all brings me to the very important topic I want to highlight: looking to the future. You need to dream, and your dreams need to be accompanied with attainable goals so that they become realities. In his song "Dreams Be Dreams" Jack Johnson has a line that says, "But girl don't let your dreams be dreams." It is a simple statement with a great truth in regards to dreaming. Too often dreams get left in the idea box where they were first stored after being created. And if that's where all of your dreams are left, nothing will become of them. Move your dreams from fantasy to reality. Take them out of the idea box.

Envision it. Plan it. Execute it. Achieve it.

In every walk of life, it is important to set goals for yourself and have dreams to work towards. And this is even more important for you with your current place in life. Having goals is what keeps you motivated. Having goals will keep you from becoming apathetic, lethargic, or feeling victimized. With goals, you can realize that you have a large amount of control over your recovery. It will change your attitude and give you a more positive outlook on this experience.

There needs to be a map or outline to follow if we are going to reach our dreams. The accomplished dream is the ultimate goal. To attain it you must first ENVISION your dream; then you must PLAN on how you will accomplish it (don't forget to take small, manageable steps); then you must EXECUTE your plan; after taking these steps you will be able to ACHIEVE it.

The same formula is used in training. When preparing to run a marathon, you don't start out on your first day of training and try to run the whole 26.2 miles. You break it up into small, obtainable goals. First you have to be able to run one mile, before you can run all 26.2 miles.

ENVISION: Envisioning your goals and dreams has a lot to do with just thinking about them. That's where all goals and dreams have to start. Before they go any further, you must internalize them. While I was in the hospital I had a lot of time to think. I had always loved sports and I consider myself to be an athletic person. Up until my liver transplant, I hadn't been able to play basketball for the past two years due to an enlarged spleen. Once I had my liver transplant, my doctors assured me that my spleen would return to normal size and I could safely play contact sports once again. As trivial as it may sound, one of the things I thought about was the type of basketball sneaker I would get once I got home from the hospital. It wasn't a major thing, but it was fun to envision the new shoes and being back on the court playing basketball with my friends.

PLAN: After you have imagined your dream or goal, you have to begin formulating a plan in order to achieve it. You may call it your strategy: the road map to achieving your goal.

One thing that may be helpful is starting a journal. I find journaling can be very therapeutic at times. It will help you keep your thoughts and ideas clear, organized, and all in one place. Laying something out on paper, whether through words or diagram, often helps bring clarity to the process.

There are two types of goals to aim for: short-term goals and long-term goals. I will explain why it is important to have both.

Short-term goals are objectives you strive to accomplish in the relatively near future. They are important because they give you drive throughout your day-to-day routine and prevent you from becoming complacent or idle. It is important that you keep both your mind and body active as much as possible during your time of healing and recovery.

A mind left alone can be a dangerous thing. I would encourage you to read, talk with people, learn something, memorize, and even watch TV or a movie (but don't watch TV or movies in large quantities). Set goals to memorize or learn something during this time if it helps. It could be Scripture, poetry, and a very practical thing to commit to memory is your list of medications. Keeping your mind sharp and active is important and will help you maintain a more positive outlook in this time.

Trying to be physically active can be tough during recovery. It requires baby steps. Push yourself, but give yourself time. You're not going to be running laps around the hospital your second week out of transplant. But setting goals such as getting out of bed on a certain day or walking around your hospital floor will help strengthen your body faster. Your doctors and nurses will most likely help you set and accomplish some of these goals. However, being proactive during your recovery goes a long way mentally and physically for your own body. It also shows your doctors that you are progressing towards being able to leave the hospital. When you take it upon yourself to accomplish something, it will strengthen your mind, boost your confidence, and help your body get everything moving internally as it should be.

After your transplant, set a goal that you can accomplish within your first week to a week and a half out of surgery and then progress toward larger goals from there. Don't set goals that are too far off that you only discourage yourself. Set small, attainable goals that you are able to reach daily and weekly. It's good to be able to see and measure your progress.

The first goal I had in mind post-transplant was simple: to play basketball again. Up until my freshman year in high school, I was a sports addict. I had played basketball and soccer and couldn't get enough of either sport until my health complications arose causing me to stop playing sports. But when I had my transplant I discovered I would be able to play basketball again. And that was my first goal to accomplish after leaving the hospital.

Long-term goals are most likely goals that you will set for yourself to be reached once you are out of the hospital. These goals will help you to keep pushing forward. However, if this becomes discouraging along the way, then set long-term goals to the side for the time being.

Long-term goals help you measure progress in greater lengths of time. As I explained, short-term goals are objectives that you can accomplish within days or a couple weeks, while long-term goals are objectives that you will aim to accomplish within several weeks, months, or even a year.

After my transplant, another goal I had was to get back in shape. In addition to just getting back in shape, however, I wanted to bulk up and gain my body's muscle back. Before becoming sick, I weighed about 175 pounds and it was something I had worked hard to obtain. After my liver transplant I dropped to 125 pounds. I realized that I had my work cut out.

119

A social worker from the hospital came into my room one day and told me that I would be granted a wish from the Make-A-Wish Foundation. I didn't choose a Disney World vacation, or a trip to the White House, or a chance to meet my favorite athlete. No, I chose to get an in-home gym. It was perfect for reaching my goal. With my exercise equipment, I was able to workout as much as I wanted and as often as I wanted. I set my goal to be a strong, 175 pounds at the one-year mark of my transplant.

As you set your goals, make sure you are able to execute your plan in a realistic time frame. If you give yourself too little time, you will become frustrated, overwhelmed, and give up. But if you give yourself too much time you run the risk of putting it off or losing focus. You might even forget about the goal all together. Depending on the size of the goal, place daily, weekly, and even monthly marks in place so that you can measure your progress along the way. Write these dates on the calendar so that you can visually track your progress.

Whether it is a short-term goal or a long-term goal, it is important that you establish the necessary steps to accomplishing them. Otherwise they will just remain an idea.

EXECUTE: You have envisioned it and planned, now do it. Put the action into your strategy and execute the plan of achieving your goal.

ACHIEVE: You have envisioned your goal, planned it, and now you are executing your plan. If you have set the necessary steps in place, you will eventually be able to see your dream become a reality. Achievement is what you have been working towards.

I've never been short on goals or dreams. In fact, I think it's very important to dream. If your dreams don't seem realistic to those around you that's okay because they're your dreams and you're the only one responsible for accomplishing them. You may have dreams of going to a certain college, running a marathon, starting a business, or living a healthy life. Whatever your dream may be, I encourage you to make a plan and execute that plan so that you can see your dream become a reality in your life.

You may encounter roadblocks along the way. You might even have to adjust the timetable to achieving your dream. But don't give up! It took Thomas Edison 10,000 failed attempts before he created his successful light bulb. Achieve your dream. Don't give up on it.

My brother and me enjoying my granted wish.

CHAPTER 7:
The Do's and Do Not's of Transplant Recovery

"Every moment and every event of every man's life on earth plants something in his soul."

-*Thomas Merton*

The do's of transplant (things to do)

From my experience of going through a transplant, there are many things I would recommend not doing. I discovered a few things along the way that only caused needless pain, added anxiety, and pointless frustration. None of which are things you need in your life at this time.

However, there are many worthwhile things you can do to help you through this experience–things that I would recommend you do. While it is not an exhaustive list, I want to provide you with a list of things for you to help pass the time, entertain yourself, keep you from needless hurt, and keep you and your mind busy while recovering in the hospital and at home. I have always appreciated suggestions from those who have already experienced what I am going through. The pathway is much clearer when you are at the end of it and looking back.

Break up the monotony

When you are traveling through the, at times, seemingly arid wasteland of recovery, it is mandatory that you give yourself something to look forward to each day. Not every day had its own large event to look forward to, but even the simple interruptions were a welcomed relief in the routinely mundane. I intentionally planned little events throughout my day to break up the monotony. For the moments that were especially long or difficult my target would help pull me through. My aim focused on things as simple as a cup of banana pudding or a bigger event like a visit from a family member. This practice may seem silly or trivial, but it proved to be very helpful in my recovery.

To this day, I still place little targets in my schedule to aim for. An event I looked forward to each day came at night when I would watch Nick at Nite while snacking on a couple handfuls of Skittles. The snack would change from time to time, but the exercise did not. I looked forward to these nights, during my recovery, when I would relax in front of the TV letting the cares of the day fade away while eating whatever snack was on the menu. Although resting and taking it easy–two essential ingredients for recovery–may seem like simple tasks, recovery was quite difficult the first days out of transplant.

It was mandatory that I stay in the surgical intensive care unit until my arterial line was taken out of my neck. After twenty-four hours in the SICU, I made it onto the liver transplant floor of the hospital. Soon after arriving I was given my first homework assignment from my coordinator: memorize the list of medications I swallowed each day. For those of you who have not been through a transplant, it is not as easy as it sounds. Pharmaceutical companies don't make it any easier with the crazy names they give these drugs. Memorizing each name, combined with the dosage I was on and the number of times I took the drug, made for one complicated list to memorize.

I soon discovered that even the most mundane events could be made somewhat enjoyable if I simply made a game out of it. Whenever possible, I would try my best to find joy even in the simple things–making the routine a little less routine. Take swallowing large amounts of pills for example. At first, you might question, "How can you find enjoyment in swallowing

30 pills in one sitting? And how is that a game?" I soon made it my own personal goal, each morning, to see how many pills I could swallow at a time. I've never had a hard time swallowing pills. I can thank my mom for the strict vitamin regime that prepared me for conquering a mountain of capsules in a fell swoop. What started as a couple small pills at the start of recovery soon turned into large handfuls at a time.

Educate yourself

In addition to breaking up the monotony, it would be to your benefit to learn as much as you can about your transplant. This is a big event in your life, so it would make sense that you learn about it. Not only for the sake of being knowledgeable about the matter at hand, but one of the greatest deterrents of fear is being educated. In my experience, I've never found ignorance to accompany bliss, so I asked as many questions as I could think of. Questions such as what to expect, time frame, possible outcomes, things I could do to help the matter, and really any question or concern that came to mind. When I was going through my liver transplant and the days that followed, I tried to learn as much as I could about each test or procedure I went through. This helped to reduce the number of surprises.

Eat

For many of us who have been through a transplant, weight loss has been a recurring theme for the past months, and maybe even years, of your life. Most likely no one will ever compel you to eat as much as you possibly can. So enjoy this time and eat what you can and, at times (when your doctor or coordinator says so), eat whatever sounds good to you. You may never find yourself in this situation again, so take advantage of it.

Journal

A great way to keep track of your thoughts and everything that's going on in your life is to keep a journal. I strongly recommend it. One day you'll be able to look back on these moments. Journaling will help keep the details from fading with time.

You can write anything and everything you want. Compile your thoughts, feelings, and even what you've been doing. As mentioned in the previous chapter, this is also a great place to write down your goals and dreams.

Take pictures

In addition to journaling, another great way to keep track of memories is to take pictures. Like climbing to the top of a mountain, it's a rewarding experience to be able to look back at what you have overcome. Even after ten years, I still enjoy being able to look back at what I've come through. I look at how frail I was in comparison to how strong I've become and feel a sense of accomplishment.

Surround yourself with positive influence

Another very beneficial practice is to surround yourself with positive influences. Maintaining a positive atmosphere for yourself is important for your psyche. There are times that your mind may be vulnerable to the negative thoughts and experiences you face. With all that you experience physically and mentally, at times, you may start to feel a weakening of both mind and will. This is why it is so important to surround yourself with a positive environment.

We have talked about it already, but it is important to keep your family and friends close in this time. Allow visitors in your room frequently, and even invite them. You will feed off the energy they bring.

I love music, and I would also encourage you to play music in your room. Whether it is played out loud through your computer, TV, or a system you have in your room or in your own headphones.

Throughout the book, you will notice that each chapter begins with a quote. These are a few of my favorite inspirational quotes I have collected over time. Some I have had for numerous years and have held on to, and others I found while I was in the hospital. If you have a few favorite quotes, write them down and keep them somewhere you will continue to see them.

If there are certain people who inspire you, whether they are athletes, authors, or family members, keep them in mind. That may include watching them on TV, reading their books, watching YouTube videos, or if you know them personally, speak with them on a regular basis.

Have something to look forward to (especially at night)

For whatever reason, I found nights to be the loneliest and some of the hardest times during recovery. For me, the nighttime brought about an unexplained sort of depression. However, I'm sure this isn't the case for everyone.

But in order to combat this, I turned nights into the most fun part of my day. My mom and I would plan out games to play, movies to watch, and, of course, Nick at Nite marathons along with all the snacks I could imagine. During this time, I may have watched every Nick at Nite show twice while eating my weight in milk shakes and popcorn.

Remember that it's the little things in life that sometimes make all the difference. While I was recovering in the hospital, I tried to come up with at least one thing to look forward to each day and that was the mail delivery. It was always exciting to see what would come in the mail, whether it was a note from a friend, a package from home, or even a card from a distant relative. Receiving mail provided both joy and encouragement for my day.

Have a place to get away

As I previously shared, I love to dream. Sometimes I read just to generate new dreams. The hospital I was in had a beautiful outside garden on the top floor, and when I was strong enough, I enjoyed taking walks to the garden to think, read, and take in the fresh air.

I encourage you to have a similar place. Have a place of solitude where you can get away from the day-to-day routine. Maybe your place to get away is just sitting by the window in your room away from your bed. Or maybe your place to get away is in the hospital cafeteria. It can be anywhere. But it is important to have a place set aside where you can escape and have a change of scenery in order to relax and think.

Take up a new hobby

Picking up a new hobby is a great way to spend the time while you are forced to slow down. Maybe you've always wanted to learn how to draw, learn a new computer program, learn a new language, have a better fantasy football team, or learn how to knit.

When you get to the point in recovery when you start feeling more like yourself again, you may find you have a large amount of time on your hands. You can only watch afternoon television for so long, so take up a new hobby. Obviously it won't work to take up rock climbing or gardening during this time, but you can start to research such hobbies so that you can start them once you are out of the hospital.

Or maybe you want to aim for a less physical hobby, one that you are able to do within the comfort of your hospital room. Choose something that will be relaxing and stress free. Don't choose a hobby that is only going to add further strain to your body during a time that your body is already under a great deal of stress. As long as you feel physically up to it, use this time to learn a new skill or begin a new hobby.

Wear your own clothes

Whenever possible, wear your own clothes. Everything around you may remind you that you are a patient recovering in a hospital, but the clothes you wear do not have to.

During my hospital stay, I had a progression of clothing. Just like everyone else, I started out wearing the not-so-dignifying hospital gown with my tail-end exposed. But during recovery, I had some of my own clothes to wear throughout the remainder of my hospital stay. The traditional gowns you're given are neither comfortable nor concealing. But wearing my own clothes was more natural and much more comfortable. It also reminded me that I had an identity beyond that of a hospital patient.

My day-to-day attire usually consisted of an oversized tank top and a baggy pair of gym shorts. However, if you choose to wear your own clothes, make sure they're not too tight so you can get in and out with ease. You also want all your lines and IV's to be accessible to your nurses. A tank top is great for pulling lines through since you don't have to worry about feeding them through a sleeve.

A close substitute for wearing your own clothes is wearing a pair of hospital scrubs as opposed to the open-back gown you are given at first. They may not be your own clothes, but at least they keep everything concealed.

Take a warm shower

You may need some help at first, and you may have to sit down while you take a shower. You may not even be able to take a traditional shower at the beginning. Your "shower" might consist of you washing yourself down with a wet towel and soap at first. But sometimes you just have to wipe off that "hospital feel." You will feel like a new person once you do.

After I had been in the hospital a couple weeks and had started to get the "hang of things", I started a morning routine. Each morning began by eating breakfast while watching television. I then took my morning medications, followed by a conversation with my doctors. After I met with my doctors, I read for a little bit and then took my daily shower or bath (also known as the time of the day when I sat in a chair and cleaned myself off with warm water, soap, and a strange shower cap pre-filled with shampoo). And then I would slip into my mid-morning nap.

Admit your fear

It may not be the most fun activity on this list of things to do, but it's worth it just the same. I can imagine you have very specific fears in mind, depending upon where you are in your journey. You might fear potential pain, uncertainty, or maybe something else that's unique to you. I want to tell you that it's okay to be afraid. Mark Twain had a great definition for courage, which is often mistaken as a lack of fear. He said courage is, "the resistance to fear, mastery of fear, not absence of fear." Too often fear is given a strong foothold in our lives, and after that, we allow it to manifest itself into something great. We end up becoming its prisoner.

I encourage you to prevent those fears from holding you captive. Admit your fear and be honest with yourself. Instead of holding it in, shed light on each one of the fears you experience. Address the fear with your coordinator, talk to your doctors, and share them with your family and friends. The more you address the fear, the more likely you are to remove the grip it has on you. Depending on the type of fear you are facing will determine how you should go about addressing it.

After you have admitted the fear to yourself, I would encourage you to write it down. It is far easier to conquer a fear that you can visualize or see on paper. After you've placed that fear on paper, attack it (I don't mean you have to poke holes in the paper itself... unless that helps). Don't allow this fear to control you, but rather conquer it with a voracious tenacity.

You may not feel comfortable enough at first, but after you've acknowledged the fear to yourself I would encourage you to go one step further: voice your fears to those around you. Let one of your close family members know and let your coordinator, doctor, and/or nurse know (don't feel like you need to tell everyone). Your support group can help provide the strength you need in the areas you are fearful.

Another great way to conquer fear is to use that fear to your advantage. Instead of it hindering you, turn the fear into a driving force. Take an athlete's fear of losing as an example. Because of the fear they have of losing, the athlete will practice and use that fear of losing as their motivation.

After my transplant one of my fears was looking like a depleted ultra-marathon runner. Rather than gracefully moving through life, my concern was that I would portray an appearance of exhaustion almost toppling over with each step. Because of this fear, I was motivated to work out. This fear of looking sickly and weak caused me to strengthen my body and get into better shape. Run at your fear with a determination that it will no longer hold you captive, but rather become your motivation. Master your fear instead of allowing it to master you.

Listen to someone's story

I love hearing the stories people have to share. I think it was something I picked up during my hospital stays when I had nowhere to go with no agenda to keep. Throughout the many moments spent in a hospital room, I heard countless stories from people passing through. Everyone has a story and I discovered that if you show yourself to be a good listener, most people are more than willing to share their story with you. Many times I've found these stories to be far more interesting than anything I could find on TV. The things I've learned and the wisdom I've received through many of these stories has been priceless.

Beware of dramatic dreams

The pain medications you're on *may* cause you to experience vivid dreams. So don't worry if your dreams seem a little more real than usual. Everyone reacts differently to pain medication and your dreams may be completely unaffected. But if you think you've awaked in the middle of the night and your hospital room has been transformed into your living room, favorite restaurant, or any other place, don't be alarmed.

If this ever happens and causes you to wake up, relax, lie down, and go back to sleep. These vivid dreams only occurred a few times during my recovery. However, it's less common than usual, and everyone's experience is unique. If this happens and causes concern, be sure to address these dreams with your transplant team.

Say "thank you"

After you've made it through surgery and have passed through the metaphorical "woods," as they say, you will find yourself in a similar place as I did. Looking back, I saw a nearly endless list of people who had helped me along the way. There were so many people to whom I was grateful. I had been nourished by the support and kind words they offered. It was often these words that carried me through the more difficult days of my transplant experience. I wish I could have taken each one of them for a cup of coffee, looked them in the eyes, and told them how much their thoughts, prayers, and encouraging words meant to me. But no matter how hard I try, I would never be able to thank them all. However, you may have the opportunity to thank many of them.

If you had an organ donated to you, I would strongly urge you to make that family your first "thank you" recipient. There are non-profit organizations that can help put you in contact with the family in an undisclosed method. I still remember writing the family of the individual I received my liver from. All I could think while writing the letter was that "thank you" wasn't nearly enough. Without their gift, I wouldn't be alive today. How do you say thank you for such a gift? But regardless, I wrote them a thank you and told them about my future plans. I wanted to let them know that their gift was going to be put to good use.

I hoped to hear back from them, but completely understood that it be hard for them to respond to such a letter. I never heard back from them and I probably will never know who they are. But I thank God for these people who have played such a vital role in my life.

Obviously you don't need me to make a list of the people deserving of your gratitude. But I would encourage you to take the time to thank those who have been your support through this time.

The do not's of transplant (things NOT to do)

There are plenty of beneficial things for you to do during your time of recovery, but there are also a few things that would be worth avoiding: the things *NOT* to do.

Do not stop taking your medications

I have already said it once, but it bears repeating: *do not stop taking your medications.* Enough said.

Do not compare

Do not compare your experience to other people's experiences. I offer you the advice and experiences from my own story as a rough outline of how things may transpire within your experience. It is natural to allow yourself to compare your experience to others, but it may cause discouragement when things do not go exactly as you had expected because you heard they went a certain way for someone else. This is *your* experience, and it will play out in your own personal way.

Comparing your journey to others is frustrating and will only discourage your outlook. Rather than entering this transplant with a preconceived idea of how everything will go, enter it with a completely open, yet determined mindset. It is okay to have somewhat of a general idea of how you think your transplant will play out. But keep yourself from comparing every detail with what you have heard of in someone else's story.

Embrace your transplant and allow it to strengthen you. Don't look at this as a weakness in your life. The strongest people I know are those who have overcome great challenges.

Do not remain silent

This means telling your doctors and nurses everything. You experience a new pain or ache somewhere: tell your nurse or doctor. You're feeling constipated: tell your nurse or doctor. You think you may need more pain medication: tell your nurse or doctor.

The more open the relationship between you and your transplant team the better off you will be. There will be times, especially at first, you won't want to discuss the number of bowel movements you've had in a day, or what color it was, but if you can talk about that, you can talk about almost anything with your nurse or doctor.

I still remember the first time my nurse walked in and asked me when the last time I had had a bowel movement. Even though I wasn't feeling up to par, I still had a sense of dignity. It was the last thing on earth I wanted to talk about. It was early on in my experience, and I wasn't accustomed to hospital culture. It didn't take long to get past this. Realize it's natural to feel this way. You aren't the first patient who hasn't wanted to discuss the color of your urine or how many bowel movements you've had. Just realize that this is part of your nurse's job and she's keeping track of these things for your own health. The sooner you can be completely open about these topics, the better.

Do not be embarrassed

After my transplant, at times I made the mistake of being embarrassed because of how physically weak I was or the scar that I now wore. At times, I allowed the scar to be a reminder of pain and saw it as a sign of limitation. But my mindset has drastically changed since then.

I am not weaker for experiencing what I did. I have become stronger because of it. Immediately following my transplant I was physically weaker for a few months. But it wasn't long before I was stronger than I had been prior to my transplant. In addition to my physical strength, I believe mentally and emotionally, I was stronger by far than when I had begun.

This experience helped shape me into who I am today. Although you may not feel physically strong at the moment, after you weather this storm, you will come out a stronger person on the other side.

Some fun ideas to keep your mind busy

The British politician, Benjamin Disraeli, once said, "Nurture your minds with great thoughts. To believe in the heroic makes heroes." Nurturing thoughts can often be difficult to come by during your recovery. You could be the most positive person and there's still a chance your thoughts won't always be heroic or constructive. I remember several difficult moments when I sat in my thoughts becoming my own recovery's worst enemy. And because of that, I want you to have a plan for when it does happen—a way to occupy your mind with positive thoughts.

Rarely do I find my mind unoccupied, but I tend to be a worrier. The simple act of worrying can be destructive to your healing progress. Because of this, I find it beneficial to have something to prevent my mind from contemplating such concerns. As a right brain person, I enjoy finding ways to improve the situation or make it more enjoyable. When I was younger, I remember trying to make games out of my chores to make them slightly more enjoyable. However, I don't think I ever came up with an idea that made dusting furniture enjoyable.

My stay in the hospital was no exception. Whether it was trying to rig my scrub pants to accommodate my drainage bags, or thinking of new ways to pass the time, I tried to squeeze every ounce of enjoyment out of opportunity I was given. The alternative of staring at the ceiling usually led to worry and frustration; I never found anything positive from either activity. The following suggestions are a few of the ideas I discovered to help pass the time and keep my mind free of nervous anxiety. Cultivate a positive mentality and keep your mind busy.

Read

What better way is there to keep your mind occupied and focused on the right track than jumping headfirst into a great book? This is a great time to catch up on reading. And if you can't think of anything to read, ask family or friends for suggestions. Just make sure that the book is both positive and entertaining. You don't need to be discouraged or bored.

Reading is a great activity for your hospital stay for many reasons. It is educational, keeps your mind active, helps you relax, and can even promote sleep.

Learn a new skill

Use this time to learn something new. You could try something more manageable like learning to write poetry, or even begin learning a new language. You could combine two activities and include how-to books in your reading.

Play games

You could play a game of I Spy with your family and friends who come and visit. You could also have someone bring board games for you to keep in your room. Your nurse may even be able to get you a couple board games from the hospital if you ask nicely. Another fun option would be hosting checkers tournaments in your room and invite your nurses, visitors, or other patients (if okayed by the staff). If these options don't sound appealing, a better option could be to make up your own game to play.

Scavenger hunt

You may have to get an okay from your nurse before trying out this next idea, but a good way to get you out of your room and moving would be to go on a scavenger hunt. Ask a family member or your nurse to make a list of things you have to find and then go find them.

Along the lines of going on a scavenger hunt, go explore the hospital. The hospital I stayed in was enormous, so I spent a lot of time just navigating the hallways. It was always nice to get out of my four walls and see something new. It may wear you out, but it will also get you ready for a solid afternoon nap.

Movie marathon

Choose your favorite trilogy, series, or collection of movies and start watching. I'm sure someone nearby can provide your beverage of choice–now all you need is someone to get you popcorn and your marathon is set to role.

Paint something

You do not even have to be an artist. Maybe this is one of the new hobbies you begin. This can become a good way to relax and release some of that built up tension.

Fantasy sports

Today there are fantasy leagues taking place all throughout the year. Personally, I've never had any success with fantasy sports. It's most likely due to the fact that I've never given it enough time. The first and last time I had a fantasy team, I felt like I had an extra full time job trying to keep up with it. However, during your recovery, you will have some time on your hands, so this might be the perfect activity for you.

Go shopping

Who says you can't shop online while lying in your hospital bed? Just because you may not get a lot of wear out of them right away doesn't mean a new pair of shoes won't put a smile on your face.

Get to know your doctor

Come up with interesting questions to ask your doctors and nurses. Ask them what their favorite movie is, where is their favorite place to vacation, or what is the strangest question they've ever been asked. Maybe you could take a poll and see who comes up with the craziest answer.

Blog

Start a blog while you are in your hospital room. You never know who might be encouraged by what you have to say.

Podcasts

Start following different podcasts.

Karaoke

As long as everyone around you is okay with it, sing your heart out.

Make a list

Make a list of all the things you are going to do and the places you are going to see when you get out of the hospital.

People watch

Find a place in the hospital with a lot of traffic and enjoy watching and listening to everything happening around you.

Last page activity

I have one last activity for you. I want you to go to the last page of this book, and depending upon the form of copy you're reading, either print it out or tear it out (I know... this is completely contrary to what your teachers and parents have told you in regards to caring for books, but I'm the author of this book and I say it's okay to tear out this one page). Now do something with it. You can do anything with it. You can even fold it up and use it as a drink coaster. But I want you to think of something creative to do with it. And then I want you to take a picture of it and then Tweet the picture to my Twitter account (@transplantdlife), or post it on my Facebook page (www.facebook.com/atransplantedlife).

CHAPTER 8:
Fight!

"Believe you can and you're half way there."

-Theodore Roosevelt

A page has been turned beginning a new chapter in your life. There's no looking back at this point, not that you would ever want to. The pain may come and go like waves tossed about in the sea. There may still be moments of doubt, and times of frustration, but as one who has weathered the storm, I can tell you that it gets better. The road to recovery can seem long and laborious at times, but there's a beautiful destination at the end of it.

At times I remember thinking to myself, "Will I ever be able to live a normal life outside these hospital walls?" There were moments I felt so dependent, worried I might run out of strength during the early days of recovery.

There will be times when you will need to remind yourself to keep going: to fight. If you experience your first bought of rejection: fight! If you are prescribed yet another medication to add to your endless list of medications you already have: fight! When your pain won't seem to quit: fight! When you have to have another CT scan and you're forced to drink the terrible tasting contrast: fight! When your general frustration seems to be getting the best of you: fight!

While discussing his training, at one point, Muhammad Ali was quoted as saying, "I hated every minute of training, but I said, 'Don't quit. Suffer now and live the rest of your life as a champion'." Consider these difficulties you're going through training for your life. Make it through these trials and you are a champion. Make it through and you undoubtedly will acquire a tenacity few will ever know. Each obstacle you overcome will prepare you for what life has to throw at you later on.

At times you may feel like you don't have any fight left, but this is why you have a support group. Gather your family and friends around you and allow them to encourage you. Allow them to uplift your spirit. The motivation they provide will help you fight to a full recovery. It's okay to be dependent and allow yourself to lean on those you hold close. Leaning on those around you in this time isn't a sign of weakness in your life. Whether it is a prayer group around you, your family hanging out in your room, or even a church group singing songs in your hospital room, this should not be a one-man battle. My Faith is what ultimately carried me through, but my family and friends were there each step of the way to keep me focused on reaching my goal.

When facing a trial, it is easy to become discouraged looking at where you are in relation to the end. But nothing is ever accomplished with one leap from start to finish. It requires progress accomplished one step at a time. Vincent Van Gogh once said, "Great things are done by a series of small things brought together." Eventually you will find yourself with only one last step from reaching your goal.

There will be a certain point when your recovery starts moving a little faster. The entire process isn't made up of small steps. It's hard to say when the moment will come because it may be gradual or it could be sudden, but one day you will notice your energy levels beginning to return and your mind becoming clearer. The great Renaissance artist, Leonardo da Vinci, once said, "Once you have tasted flight you will walk the earth with your eyes turned skywards, for there you have been and there you will long to return." Your health is your flight, and you tasted it before you were sick. You know what it is like to feel strong and free from pain.

As I stated at the beginning of this book, it's not my goal to provide you with an example to compare your experience. My hope is that I have provided you with a resource to explain some of the experiences you may go through.

Never tell yourself that you can't do it. You can. And if you continue to tell yourself you can, then you will. Keep your support group close; set goals for yourself; fight your way to those goals; and you will become a stronger healthier version of yourself.

Further Resources

It's not an exhaustive list, but I've compiled a list of a few resources that might be assistance during your transplant. Several of these organizations helped me during my transplant.

Before my transplant, we realized we were going to have to make some unique travel arrangements due to the distance between where I lived and where I was having my transplant. We wouldn't be able to make the drive from Des Moines, Iowa to Saint Louis, Missouri in the appropriate amount of time when the call came in. I was fortunate enough to be connected to Angel Flight by my coordinator. Angel Flight is an amazing non-profit group composed of pilots who offer their services and planes to those in need of legitimate medical travel assistance. Angel Flight made the most gracious accommodations in order to pick me up at the nearest airstrip and deliver me to the airport closest to my hospital. This group of pilots and the individuals who support them proved to be an invaluable blessing to so many others and me. To learn more about this non-profit organization, visit their website at www.AngelFlight.com

When seeking resources, your first outlet should be your transplant social worker at your hospital. This person can help direct you to the appropriate resources that would be most beneficial for your particular case or concern. They can also help you get signed up for different financial aid programs or medical cost assistance programs if needed. Most of the time social worker can look to see what programs are still available at any given point in the year. A lot of these programs are offered through grant programs, some from the government and some from other means. Often they are set up on a first come first serve basis to those that qualify.

For those of you taking tacrolimus (the brand name is Prograf), it would be worth looking into the Prograf Value Card. It is simple to sign up and they help cover a portion of your Prograf prescription each month. However, if your prescription is already being paid by a state or federal program they will not offer payment.

Astellas Access is a wealth of financial information. They offer the Prograf Value Card (powered by McKesson) and many other programs on their website at www.AstellasAccess.com.

There are many programs to be discussed and do not be discouraged just because one turns you down when you apply. Below is a list of a few other outlets to explore.

Further support and other resources:

Join a support group: I would encourage you to join your hospital's transplant support group or find one in your local area. Within this group, you will be able to speak with patients who have gone through this experience already and ask any questions you may have. If you can't find one locally, join an online forum. There's comfort in being able to communicate with those who have experienced what you are going through. There are some things that your family and friends won't be able to understand. If they haven't gone through an organ transplant, they simply can't relate to much of what you go through. Ask your transplant coordinator for more information about your hospital's support group or assistance in putting you in contact with one close to home.

American Transplant Foundation
www.AmericanTransplantFoundation.org

American Liver Foundation
www.LiverFoundation.org

U.S. Department of Health & Human Services Organ Donor
www.OrganDonor.gov

Transplant Friends
www.TransplantFriends.com
Transplant Friends and Transplant Buddies (listed below) are two great outlets for transplant patients seeking support and to find further resources and answers. Even if you don't have a desire to become an active part of the community they've established, I would strongly recommend that you sign up for their newsletter.

Transplant Buddies
www.TransplantBuddies.org

Children's Liver Association for Support Services (C.L.A.S.S.)
www.CLASSKids.org

One Legacy
www.OneLegacy.org

Genentech
www.gene.com

Novartis Pharmaceutical Corporation
www.MyFortic.com

OPTN (Organ Procurement and Transplantation Network)
optn.transplant.hrsa.gov

Ronald McDonald House Charities
www.RMHC.org
www.RMHCSTL.com (The St. Louis Ronald McDonald House Charity)
Ronald McDonald House Charities helps families find strength in numbers through a network of local Chapters. These Chapters, which can be found in 58 countries and regions across the globe, provide a "home-away-from-home" for families of seriously ill children.

Transplant Recipients International Organization (TRIO)
www.TrioWeb.org

Second Wind Lung Transplant Association, Inc.
www.2ndWind.org

Financial assistance:

There are plenty of other financial resources that are available. These are just a few options to start with. You may consider doing some research on your own. However, be sure to speak with your hospital financial caseworker or transplant social worker to see if they may be aware of any grants or funds that could benefit you. In regards to your medications, speak with your pharmacist and ask if they are aware of any pharmaceutical programs or discount cards that could help with your prescriptions.

American Transplant Foundation
www.AmericanTransplantFoundation.org

Astellas Access
www.AstellasAccess.com

GiveForward
www.giveforward.com
GiveForward is the nation's only online fundraising platform dedicated to helping individuals create personal fundraising pages to help cover their medical bills and out-of-pocket expenses. Go to www.GiveForward.com to create a free page, and then share the link to this page with friends and family so they can donate to your expenses, leave messages of support and stay up-to-date on your progress before, during and after a transplant.

Health Well Foundation
www.HealthWellFoundation.org
1-800-675-8416

National Foundation for Transplants
www.transplants.org

National Transplant Assistance Fund
www.ntafund.org

Patient Access Network (PAN) Foundation
www.PanFoundation.org
866-316-PANF

Patient Assistance Program for Organ Transplant
www.pparx.org
1-800-477-6472

RX Hope
www.RxHope.com
1-877-267-0517

True RX Savings
www.TrueRXSavings.com
1-800-886-8412

Transplant FAQ

NOTE FROM THE AUTHOR: Every organ transplant case is unique and there are many variables to consider. Every question should be directed toward your doctor and organ transplant team.

Kidney

What is the donor surgery like?
You will be admitted in the hospital the morning of surgery and you will go through a physical examination, including blood work, chest X-ray, and EKG. If all goes well, you will be okay for surgery, but there are times that the patient has been sent home. If you pass the physical exam, the doctor will administer you IV fluids and answer your remaining questions. You will then be escorted to surgery and the anesthesiologist will sedate you. Once you are fully asleep, you will be given a breathing tube to help you breathe during surgery and a catheter will be placed into your bladder. The surgery then begins.

What happens during transplant surgery?
Shortly before going into surgery, medicine is given to the patients to help them relax. A general anesthetic is then given. The donor and recipient are in adjacent operating rooms. The transplant surgeon removes the kidney from the donor and prepares it for transplant into the recipient. There, the surgeon connects the renal artery and vein of the new kidney to the recipient's artery and vein. This creates blood flow through the kidney, which makes urine. The ureter, or tube coming down from the donor kidney, is sewn into the bladder. Usually, the new kidney will start

working right away. Sometimes, it takes several days for the donor kidney to "wake up."

How long is the transplant surgery?
The surgery generally takes up to 2-3 hours.

How long will I be in the hospital following my transplant?
Patients typically spend from three to seven days in the hospital following kidney transplant surgery.

How far away (from the hospital) can I live while I wait?
You will need to be close enough that you can get to the hospital within 2 ½ hours of being called, either by car or airplane.

Can I travel while I am on the waiting list?
Under most circumstances: please consult with your transplant coordinator prior to making travel arrangements.

Will I need to take medications for the rest of my life?
Yes. To attempt to prevent your body from rejecting your new kidney, you will need to take immunosuppressive medications daily for the rest of your life. These medications play a crucial role in keeping your new heart working properly.

How long will I wait for my transplant?
See UNOS, MELD and PELD in chapter 2 of part 1

How many kidney transplants happen each year?
In 2012, 16,487 kidney transplants were performed.

Heart

What happens during the transplant operation?
Before the surgery begins, you will be put into a deep sleep by general anesthesia. An incision is then made in the chest through the breastbone. Your diseased heart will be removed and in its place the surgeons will

stitch the new and healthy heart. The blood vessels of your old heart will be reconnected to the donor heart, which should then warm up and begin to beat. If this is not the case, then the surgeon will try to start your new heart with an electric shock. During the entire process, you will be connected to a heart-lung bypass machine that does the heart's work while yours is stopped during surgery. It sends out enough blood and oxygen throughout your body to keep your blood circulating. Once your new donor heart begins to beat, you will then be taken off of this machine. After surgery, tubes are entered into the chest to drain out any air, fluids, or blood, allowing the lungs to re-expand over several days. You may also be administered medication for a few days to help you sustain a regular heartbeat.

Another type of heart transplant that may be performed is a heterotopic transplant. In this type, the surgeon will typically place the new heart on top of the old heart and just join them together.

How long is the transplant operation?
Heart transplant surgery usually takes about four hours — longer if you've had previous heart surgeries or if there are complications during the procedure.

How long will I be in the hospital following my transplant?
This can vary from person to person. However, most people are in the hospital from 10 to 14 days. Generally, you'll be in the Intensive Care Unit two to three days and on the general cardiac surgery division for seven to 10 days.

How far away (from the hospital) can I live while I wait?
You will need to be close enough that you can get to the hospital within 2 ½ hours of being called, either by car or airplane.

Can I travel while I am on the waiting list?
Under most circumstances: please consult with your transplant coordinator prior to making travel arrangements.

How long will I wait for my transplant?
See UNOS, MELD and PELD in chapter 2 of part 1

How many heart transplants happen each year?
In 2012, 2,378 heart transplants were performed.

Lung

What happens before surgery?
You will wait in the transplant unit until the final results of the cross match are determined. If the cross match results are negative (or compatible) and the on-site organ procurement team indicates the organ is of good quality, you will be prepared for surgery (generally within a few hours of your admission).

What happens during surgery?
An anesthesiologist will inject general anesthesia (pain-relieving medicine) through your IV, which will make you go to sleep. After you are asleep:

- A central venous catheter is inserted into a vein in your neck or groin. This type of catheter is used to deliver fluids, nutrition solutions, antibiotics, or blood products directly into your bloodstream without frequently having to insert a needle into your vein.
- A tube is placed in your mouth that goes down your throat and into your windpipe (trachea) to help you breathe. The tube is attached to a ventilator that will expand your lungs mechanically.
- You might be placed on a heart/lung machine to allow surgeons to bypass the blood flow to the heart and lungs. The machine pumps blood through the body, removing carbon dioxide (a waste product) and replacing it with oxygen needed by body tissues.
- A nasogastric tube is inserted through your nose into your stomach.
- A tube called a catheter is placed in your bladder to drain urine.
- The surgeon carefully removes your lung and replaces it with the donor lung.

How long is the transplant surgery?
The procedure lasts about six hours. Family members and friends are invited to wait for you in the Family Waiting Lounge until the surgery is completed. We ask visitors to sign in and out of the waiting area and provide a phone number so we can contact them if necessary. A member of the transplant team will meet with your family in the waiting area to keep them updated on the progress of your surgery. Your family will be notified when the surgery is complete and when they can visit you in the intensive care unit.

How long will I be in the hospital following my transplant?
This can vary from person to person. However, most people are in the hospital from 10 to 14 days. Generally, this includes one to two days in the cardiothoracic surgery intensive care unit and 7 to 10 days on the general thoracic surgery division.

How far away (from the hospital) can I live while I wait?
You will need to be close enough that you can get to the hospital within 2 ½ hours of being called, either by car or airplane.

Can I travel while I am on the waiting list?
Under most circumstances: please consult with your transplant coordinator prior to making travel arrangements.

How long will I wait for my transplant?
See UNOS, MELD and PELD in chapter 2 of part 1

How many lung transplants happen each year?
In 2012, 1754 lung transplants were performed.

Liver

What is the donor surgery like?
During living donor liver transplant surgery, the donor begins surgery first. Using the split-liver technique, the surgeon removes a portion of the donor's liver and prepares it for transplant. Then, another surgical team

removes your diseased liver, replacing it with the portion of liver from the living donor.

The living donor's liver regenerates to full size within a few weeks of the surgery, and there is no long-term impairment of liver function. The transplanted liver portion also regenerates, increasing until it's the appropriate size for your body.

The donor spends about a week in the hospital recovering, and should plan for two to three months off work. For the recipient, post-transplant care and follow-up is the same as for a deceased donor liver transplant.

What happens during the transplant operation?

During the operation, surgeons will remove your liver and will replace it with the donor liver. Because a transplant operation is a major procedure, surgeons will need to place several tubes in your body. These tubes are necessary to help your body carry out certain functions during the operation and for a few days afterward.

- During the operation, a tube will be placed through your mouth into your windpipe (trachea) to help you breathe during the operation and for the first day or two following the operation. The tube is attached to a ventilator that will expand your lungs mechanically.
- A nasogastric tube will be inserted through your nose into your stomach. The nasogastric tube will drain secretions from your stomach, and it will remain in place for a few days until your bowel function returns to normal.
- A tube called a catheter will be placed in your bladder to drain urine. This will be removed a few days after the operation.
- Three tubes will be placed in your abdomen to drain blood and fluid from around the liver. These will remain in place for about one week.

In some cases, the surgeon will place a special tube, called a T-tube, in your bile duct. The T-tube will drain bile into a small pouch outside of your body so it can be measured several times daily. Only certain transplant patients receive a T-tube, which remains in place for five months. The tube causes no discomfort and does not interfere with daily activities.

How long is the transplant surgery?
Liver transplants usually take from 6 to 12 hours (this may sound like a wide range, but there are many factors to consider in a liver transplant surgery).

How long will I be in the hospital following the transplant?
The ranges vary.

How far away (from the hospital) can I live while I wait?
Usually, there are not restrictions on where patients waiting for a liver can live, but they must have arrangements made so they can arrive at the hospital within six hours.

Can I travel while I am on the waiting list?
Under most circumstances: please consult with your transplant coordinator prior to making travel arrangements.

How long will I wait for my transplant?
See UNOS, MELD and PELD in chapter 2 of part 1

How many liver transplants happen each year?
In 2012, 6,256 liver transplants were performed in the United States.

Pancreas

What happens during the transplant operation?
Surgeons perform pancreas transplants during general anesthesia, so you're unconscious during the procedure. The anesthesiologist or anesthetist gives you an anesthetic medication as a gas to breathe through a mask or injects a liquid medication into a vein.

The surgical team monitors your heart rate, blood pressure and blood oxygen throughout the procedure with a blood pressure cuff on your arm and heart-monitor leads attached to your chest. After you're unconscious:

- An incision is made down the center of your abdomen.
- The surgeon places the new pancreas and a small portion of the donor's small intestine into your lower abdomen.
- The donor intestine is attached to either your small intestine or your bladder, and the donor pancreas is connected to blood vessels that also supply blood to your legs.
- Your own pancreas is left in place to aid digestion.
- If you're also receiving a kidney transplant, the blood vessels of the new kidney will be attached to blood vessels in the lower part of your abdomen.
- The new kidney's ureter — the tube that links the kidney to the bladder — will be connected to your bladder. Unless your own kidneys are causing complications, such as high blood pressure or infection, they're left in place.

Pancreas transplant surgery usually lasts about three hours, but the duration varies depending on different factors. Simultaneous kidney-pancreas transplant surgery takes a few more hours.

After a pancreas transplant
After your pancreas transplant, you can expect to:

- **Stay in the intensive care unit for a few days.** Doctors and nurses monitor your condition to watch for signs of complications. Your new pancreas should start working immediately, and your old pancreas will continue to perform its other functions. If you have a new kidney, it'll make urine just like your own kidneys did when they were healthy. Often this starts immediately. But in some cases, urine production takes up to a few weeks.
- **Spend about one week in the hospital.** Once you're stable, you're taken to a transplant recovery area to continue recuperating. Expect soreness or pain around the incision site while you're healing.

- **Have frequent checkups as you continue recovering.** After you leave the hospital, close monitoring is necessary for three to four weeks. Your transplant team will develop a checkup schedule that's right for you. During this time, if you live in another town, you may need to make arrangements to stay close to the transplant center.
- **Take lifelong medications.** You'll take a number of medications after your pancreas transplant. Drugs called immunosuppressants help keep your immune system from attacking your new pancreas. Additional drugs may help reduce the risk of other complications, such as infection and high blood pressure, after your transplant.

How long is the transplant surgery?
The ranges vary.

How long will I be in the hospital following the transplant?
The average post transplant hospital stay is about two weeks.

How far away (from the hospital) can I live while I wait?
Usually, there are not restrictions on where patients waiting for a pancreas can live, but they must have arrangements made so they can arrive at the hospital within six hours.

Can I travel while I am on the waiting list?
Under most circumstances: please consult with your transplant coordinator prior to making travel arrangements.

How long will I wait for my transplant?
See UNOS, MELD and PELD in chapter 2 of part 1

How many pancreas transplants happen each year?
In 2012, 1,043 pancreas transplants were performed in the United States.

Intestine

What happens during the transplant operation?

Although it is possible for a living donor to donate an intestine segment, most intestine transplants involve a whole organ from a deceased donor. In addition, most intestine transplants are performed in conjunction with a liver transplant.

Depending on your condition, the transplant team will perform one of the following surgeries:

Isolated intestine transplantation

Your surgeons will remove a diseased portion of the small intestine and replace it with a healthy small intestine from a deceased donor. This type of transplantation will be performed if you suffer only from intestinal failure.

Liver–intestine transplantation

You may need a transplantation of both the small intestine and liver at the same time. This type of surgery is performed if both the liver and intestine have failed.

Multivisceral transplantation

This is a transplantation of the small intestine along with other organs that have failed, such as the stomach, pancreas or kidney.

How long is the transplant surgery?

The ranges vary.

How long will I be in the hospital following the transplant?

The ranges vary.

How far away (from the hospital) can I live while I wait?

Usually, there are not restrictions on where patients waiting for an intestine can live, but they must have arrangements made so they can arrive at the hospital within six hours.

Can I travel while I am on the waiting list?
Under most circumstances: please consult with your transplant coordinator prior to making travel arrangements.

How long will I wait for my transplant?
See UNOS, MELD and PELD in chapter 2 of part 1

How many intestine transplants happen each year?
In 2012, 106 intestine transplants were performed in the United States.

Thank you...

A popular line in Meditation XVII from John Donne's *Devotions Upon Emergent Occasions* states, "No man is an island." The 17th century poet was referring to the connection we have with the people around us. While writing this book, and reflecting back over the past decade of my life, I have acquired a more accurate appreciation for the truth within this simple phrase.

Seclusion, no matter how tropical the location might be, is a lonely, difficult place. As humans we rarely operate very well on our own. Without the love and interaction of the relationships around us, we would never make it far. I'd be delusional to say I made it through on my own. When I look at where I am and the distance I've covered, I look back and see an endless list of individuals who have helped me get to where I am today.

It's an endless list, but here are a few of the people that deserve a great deal of acknowledgement and thanks.

I thank God for my dad who I thought of so often while writing this book. I can't wait to swap stories with him some day in heaven. From everything I've been told, he poured his love into the first two years of my life while holding nothing back.

I thank my beautiful wife who experienced the writing of this book along with me. She became my constant editor telling me when to let go of an unneeded sentence or paragraph that served no purpose; sitting with me as I recalled some of the more painful moments of my experience; and being a constant source of encouragement.

I want to thank my parents. My mom who never left my side during my many many hospital stays. And so much further beyond her physical presence, she's been a constant source of encouragement and prayer throughout my entire life. To my stepdad for supporting me through the trials of life and for supporting Mom as we all walked through those trials together.

I thank my siblings who've all been an encouragement in their own individual way: Nate, my big brother, who's had my back through every stage of life and specifically for being a greatly needed encouragement many times throughout my transplant. Sarah, for being a part of my send-off party on the tarmac. Nat, for caring so much that you were willing to risk your own life and volunteer to become my living donor. There's not a "thank you" big enough to offer in return for that kind of love. Hannah, for being a blessing then and now and playing the role as one of this book's editors even during pregnancy. To the rest of my siblings: thank you for your constant prayers and encouragement.

To Pat Rolfe, my editor, mentor, friend, and sometimes my Nashville mom. Even beyond grammar I have learned so much from you. You've shown me what true, southern tenacity looks like, the correct definition and spelling of *possessed,* and so much more.

If it were not for my doctors I wouldn't be standing here today. Without a doubt in my mind, I had the greatest team of doctors walking me through this journey. The first doctor that comes to mind was my transplant doctor and the author of this book's forward, Dr. Ross Shepherd. He is a man who deserves every compliment each of his patients and parents of those patients have given him. As I mentioned in the book, my God-given peace was delivered by way of Dr. Shepherd. Dr. Shepherd, thank you.

Dr. Lowell, I thank you for being straightforward and for not getting carried away with the coating of sugar on difficult news you sometimes had to deliver. In addition to the medical care you provided, I greatly appreciate your support in making this book a reality.

Dr. Horslen, I thank you for having the foresight to see what so many had overlooked. Dr. Desai, I thank you for being another great example of a doctor who saw his patients as more than a file and took the time to invest in me personally. Dr. Turmelle, thank you for being the ray of sunshine in the often dreary days of recovery.

Unless you've gone through a transplant, you may not know how important transplant coordinators are to their patients. When I say that these two ladies were like mothers to me, I say that in the most endearing way possible. Lyn, thank you for not only putting up with me and my inability to remember the names and dosages of my list of medications as we recited them each afternoon, but for also putting up with my mother, who, we can all admit was not the easiest parent to cope with. And Michelle, I want to thank you for telling me when to pick myself up and try again—for never allowing me fail in recovery.

To each and every nurse that I've been blessed to fall under the care of, I say *thank you.* But to the one nurse, in particular, I want to thank—Ozzy. You took the time to get to know your patients better than anyone else. I can't think of any other nurse who has cared enough to bring pillows from outside the hospital because of his patient's particular sleeping arrangements.

To my friend, Joseph McLean Gregory: if it had not been for your support, this book may not have happened. The direction and positive feedback you provided were the wings to the idea I had developed.

To David, for your friendship that has stood the test of time. And for your creative, humorous spin you place on life—thank you.

To Matt, for allowing me to pick your brain, for your encouragement since day one, and for believing in my ideas—thank you.

To Mark, for your advice and support and for the blessing you've been both intentionally and unintentionally—thank you.

To Austin, the funniest and one of the most genuine guys I know, thank you for providing my life with a constant healthy dose of humor.

Charlie, it's an honor to call you a friend. I have a great amount of respect for what you've done in life and I appreciate the influence you had on this book.

And most of all, I thank my Lord and Savior, Jesus Christ, for my second chance at life.

And to the endless list of others who have supported, encouraged, and prayed for me along the way, I want to thank you. To my aunts, uncles, cousins, other family members, and friends—thank you.

Credits

Editor: Pat Rolfe
Editor: Hannah Jackson
Editor: Ella Marie Wilson

Book cover photography: Ryan Francois

Additional Thanks

Jerry Bauer
Mark and Lindsay Mattingly
Matt and Erica Yezerski
Tyler and Sarah Anderson
Larry and Sherry Nemmers
Jerry and Marian Malek
Paul and Connie Swanson
Joe Mellone

Bibliography

p. 15   Autoimmune Hepatitis. (2011, October 4). *American Liver Foundation*. Retrieved October 3, 2013, from http://www. liverfoundation.org/abouttheliver/info/aihep/

p. 21   MELD Score. (n.d.). *United Network for Organ Sharing*. Retrieved October 3, 2013, from http://www.unos.org/docs/ MELD_PELD.pdf

p. 33   Transplant Q and A. (2014, April 10). *Transplant Q and A*. Retrieved October 3, 2014, from http://www.liverfoundation.org/ education/liverlowdown/ll0414/transplantq/

p. 53   Barnes Jewish Hospital (getting to the hospital within 6 hours of receiving the call)

Interviews

Horslen, Dr. Simon. Personal interview. 14 Feb. 2013.

Shepherd, Dr. Ross. Personal interview. 25 May 2013.

Lowell, Dr. Jeffrey. Personal interview. 31 July 2013.

Nemmers, Marilyn. Personal interview. 1 Oct. 2013.

Page, Melody. Personal interview. 2 Oct. 2013.

Desai, Dr. Niraj. Personal interview. 28 Oct. 2013.

Bianchi, Lyn. Personal interview. 2 Dec. 2013.

Wittmack, Charlie. Personal interview. 1 Feb. 2014.

Yezerski, Dr. Matthew. Personal interview. 11 July 2014.

Quotes

Liver Foundation
http://www.liverfoundation.org/abouttheliver/info/aihep/
Page updated: October 4th, 2011
(referenced on page 15)

UNOS
Unos.org
http://www.unos.org/docs/MELD_PELD.pdf
(Long quotation from UNOS)
10/3/13

Liver Foundation
liverfoundation.org
("The average liver transplant lasts anywhere from 3 to 7 hours depending
on the details of the operation" –page 33)

Transplant FAQ:

Kidney

What is the donor surgery like?
What happens during transplant surgery?
Barnes-Jewish Hospital | St. Louis, MO | National Leaders in Medicine.
(n.d.). Barnes-Jewish Hospital. Retrieved July 19, 2014, from
http://www.barnesjewish.org/kidney-transplant

How long is the transplant surgery?

American Transplant Foundation. (n.d.). American Transplant Foundation. Retrieved July 17, 2014, from http://www.americantransplantfoundation.org/

How long will I be in the hospital following my transplant?
How far away (from the hospital) can I live while I wait?
Can I travel while I am on the waiting list?

Barnes-Jewish Hospital | St. Louis, MO | National Leaders in Medicine. (n.d.). Barnes-Jewish Hospital. Retrieved July 19, 2014, from http://www.barnesjewish.org/kidney-transplant

How many kidney transplants happen each year?

OPTN/SRTR 2012 Annual Data Report. (n.d.). OPTN/SRTR Annual Report. Retrieved July 18, 2014, from http://srtr.transplant.hrsa.gov/annual_reports/2012/pdf/04_intestine_13.pdf OPTN & SRTR Annual Data Report 2012

Heart

What happens during the transplant operation?

American Transplant Foundation. (n.d.). American Transplant Foundation. Retrieved July 17, 2014, from http://www.americantransplantfoundation.org/

How long is the transplant operation?

Staff, M. (2010, December 10). Heart transplant. Mayo Clinic. Retrieved July 19, 2014, from http://www.mayoclinic.com/health/heart-transplant/MY00361/DSECTION=what-you-can-expect

How long will I be in the hospital following my transplant?
How far away (from the hospital) can I live while I wait?
Can I travel while I am on the waiting list?

Barnes-Jewish Hospital | St. Louis, MO | National Leaders in Medicine. (n.d.). Barnes-Jewish Hospital. Retrieved July 19, 2014, from http://www.barnesjewish.org/heart-transplant

How many heart transplants happen each year?
OPTN/SRTR 2012 Annual Data Report. (n.d.). OPTN/SRTR Annual Report. Retrieved July 18, 2014, from http://srtr.transplant.hrsa.gov/ annual_reports/2012/pdf/04_intestine_13.pdf OPTN & SRTR Annual Data Report 2012

Lung

What happens before surgery?
What happens during surgery?
How long is the transplant surgery?
How long will I be in the hospital following my transplant?
How far away (from the hospital) can I live while I wait?
Can I travel while I am on the waiting list?
Barnes-Jewish Hospital | St. Louis, MO | National Leaders in Medicine.
    (n.d.). Barnes-Jewish Hospital. Retrieved July 19, 2014, from
    http://www.barnesjewish.org/lung-transplant-process

How many lung transplants happen each year?
OPTN/SRTR 2012 Annual Data Report. (n.d.). OPTN/SRTR Annual Report. Retrieved July 18, 2014, from http://srtr.transplant.hrsa.gov/ annual_reports/2012/pdf/04_intestine_13.pdf OPTN & SRTR Annual Data Report 2012

Liver

What is the donor surgery like?
American Transplant Foundation. (n.d.). American Transplant
    Foundation. Retrieved July 17, 2014, from http://www.
    americantransplantfoundation.org/

What happens during the transplant operation?
How long is the transplant surgery?
How long will I be in the hospital following the transplant?
How far away (from the hospital) can I live while I wait?
Can I travel while I am on the waiting list?

Barnes-Jewish Hospital | St. Louis, MO | National Leaders in Medicine. (n.d.). Barnes-Jewish Hospital. Retrieved July 19, 2014, from http://www.barnesjewish.org/liver-transplant

How many liver transplants happen each year?
OPTN/SRTR 2012 Annual Data Report. (n.d.). OPTN/SRTR Annual Report. Retrieved July 18, 2014, from http://srtr.transplant.hrsa.gov/annual_reports/2012/pdf/04_intestine_13.pdf OPTN & SRTR Annual Data Report 2012

Pancreas

What happens during the transplant operation?
After a pancreas transplant
How long is the transplant surgery?
How long will I be in the hospital following the transplant?
Pancreas transplant. (n.d.). What you can expect. Retrieved July 19, 2014, from http://www.mayoclinic.org/tests-procedures/pancreas-transplant/basics/what-you-can-expect/prc-20014239

How many pancreas transplants happen each year?
OPTN/SRTR 2012 Annual Data Report. (n.d.). OPTN/SRTR Annual Report. Retrieved July 18, 2014, from http://srtr.transplant.hrsa.gov/annual_reports/2012/pdf/04_intestine_13.pdf OPTN & SRTR Annual Data Report 2012

Intestine

What happens during the transplant operation?
Transplant Living | About the Operation | Intestine. (n.d.). Transplant Living | About the Operation | Intestine. Retrieved July 19, 2014, from http://www.transplantliving.org/before-the-transplant/about-the-operation/intestine/

What to Expect If Your Child Needs an Intestine Transplant. (n.d.). Seattle Children's Hospital. Retrieved July 19, 2014, from http://www.seattlechildrens.org/clinics-programs/transplant/intestine/what-to-expect-if-your-child-needs-an-intestine-transplant/

How long is the transplant surgery?

How long will I be in the hospital following the transplant?

How far away (from the hospital) can I live while I wait?

What to Expect If Your Child Needs an Intestine Transplant. (n.d.). Seattle Children's Hospital. Retrieved July 19, 2014, from http://www.seattlechildrens.org/clinics-programs/transplant/intestine/what-to-expect-if-your-child-needs-an-intestine-transplant/

Can I travel while I am on the waiting list?

What to Expect If Your Child Needs an Intestine Transplant. (n.d.). Seattle Children's Hospital. Retrieved July 19, 2014, from http://www.seattlechildrens.org/clinics-programs/transplant/intestine/what-to-expect-if-your-child-needs-an-intestine-transplant/

How many intestine transplants happen each year?

OPTN/SRTR 2012 Annual Data Report. (n.d.). OPTN/SRTR Annual Report. Retrieved July 18, 2014, from http://srtr.transplant.hrsa.gov/annual_reports/2012/pdf/04_intestine_13.pdf OPTN & SRTR Annual Data Report 2012

About the Author

Noah Swanson received his liver transplant over ten years ago at the age of sixteen. He has a background in product development that indirectly fueled his desire to share the story of his journey through organ transplant. He now lives in Iowa with his wife and two daughters (London is three and their second daughter is due in September of 2015) where he continues to pursue life to the fullest.

#ATransplantedLife
@A_Transplanted_life